Image of Reflection

Image of Reflection

Volume 1

Written by

Roger Egner

Contributing Writers
Joshua Egner – a Book that is
Taylor Egner – Cosmic Herald

Things to be mindful of:

When using this material, it is recommended that the user create an environment where s/he will not be disturbed or distracted. This product is for entertainment purposes and personal use only and is distributed "as is" without warranties of any kind.

Paperback ISBN: 978-0-578-08081-9
Hardcover ISBN: 978-0-578-08082-6

For all the G_od souls of the realm

Gateway to the Realm

Reference Cards

PAGE # CARD NAME

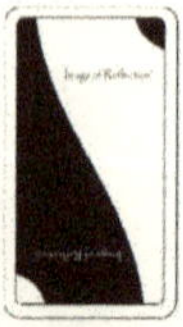

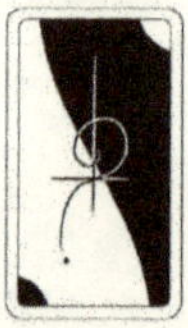

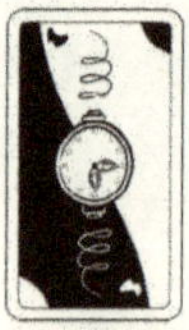

Gateway to the Realm

Reference Cards

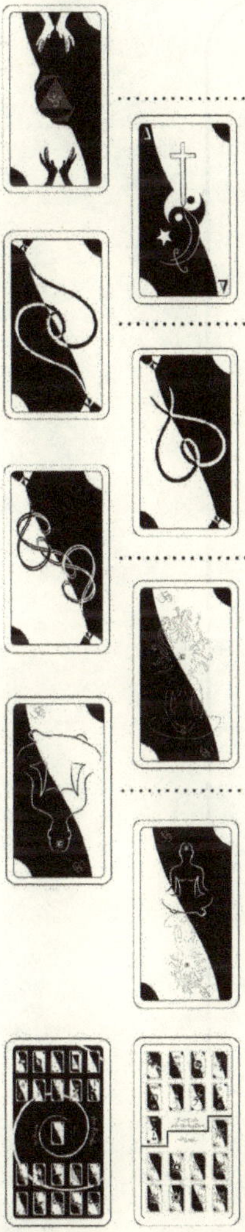

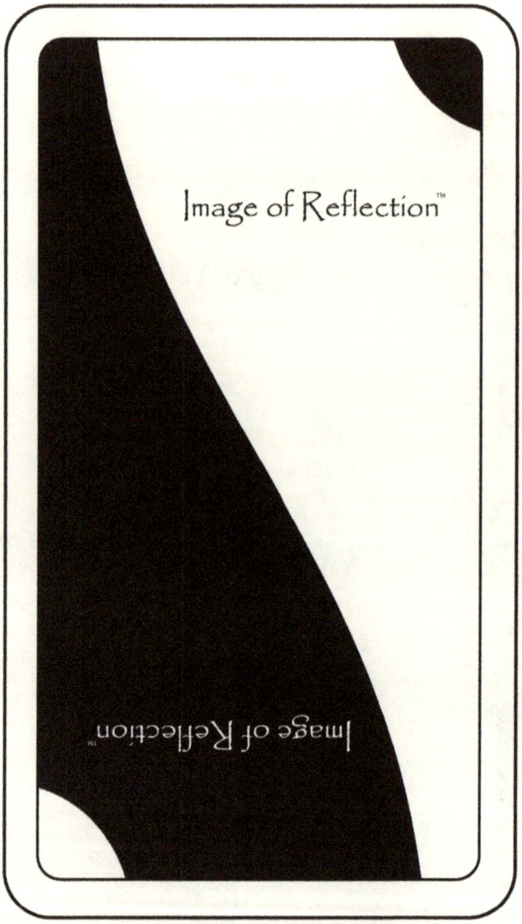

Entrance Portal

Sub-deck: Story

Entrance Portal

A mirror image of what's next.

What's at risk to gaze into a mirror seeking a reflection?

Some-thing you may think, no-thing you kno for sure, every-thing beyond what One can think to imagine coming insight.

In the end it's not knoing… that matters, as well as the courage of your faith to look deeper beyond any-thing religiously held onto in fear.

It only takes three slow deep breaths to wonder within and just one in YinYang to out "think" your-self.

Imagine that… and "it" will soon appear.

Peace and Courage to all beings of the realm

Aigh...

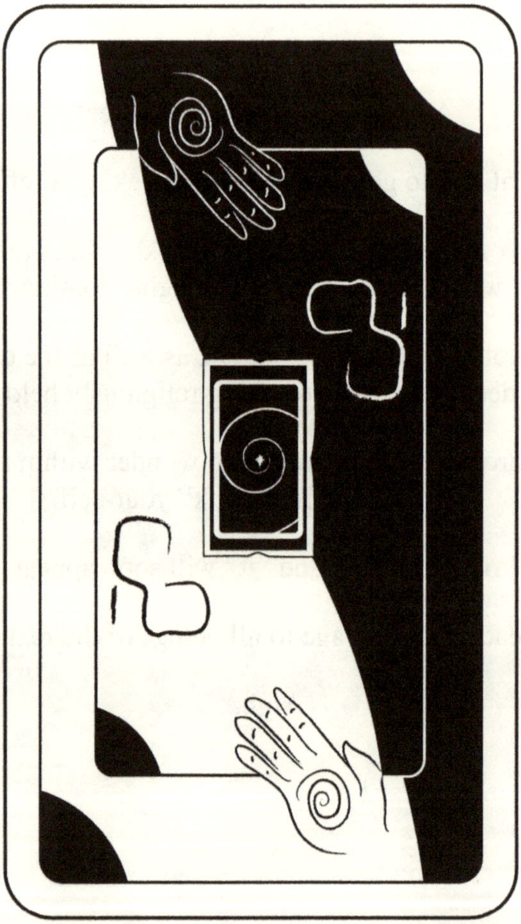

Guest Reading

Sub-deck: Readings

Guest Reading

Whapuuuuuu… Ha…

One may hear some-thing odd to the ear that sounds tricky yet no-thing is a trick. Every-thing One may think of "things" like this is nothing that can't be imagined in YinYang. How One chooses to judge "things" is but a mirror reflection of their own G_od faith. One has but to wonder into the cards to see the G_od sense in what's being said on balance – truth.

So, what's the point? It's not knoing… getting there is a One of a kind journey played out in the cards dealt by One's own hand in G_od faith. Fore in the Realm all spirits really do choose…

It's what's next.

Imagine that…

Ha… Whapuuuuu…

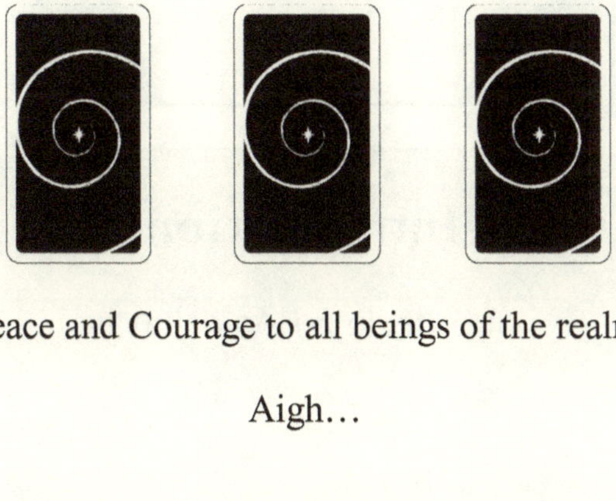

Peace and Courage to all beings of the realm

Aigh…

Introduction

Sub-deck: a Book that is

Introduction

It could be said that this introduction is an attempt to bridge the gap of insanity that some may face when they are confronted with my father's work. For he speaks a different language than all of us, and only he has the luxury of being a native speaker. I am but a translator that, through close contact and observation, has come to glean some meaning from his words.

The cynics out there, and perhaps those who have read ahead unguided, are wondering, why bother with this Crazy Buffalo and his crazy talk? To them I can give no straight answer, or unconditional justification, of why anyone goes around using the words that they do. In the end, however, it boils down to significance, that you use your words to convey an idea. As I am doing now, and you do every day in whatever tongue you speak, and in this much we communicate, with common names born from ideas. If, just perhaps, this Crazy Buffalo were to have a new idea, it certainly would exist as much as those others with names, but lacking one, its founder created a name, in hopes that it may be communicated, and so is born a word, and a language.

This book is a discourse on, and in, that language, written by its creator, in hopes that it may open new perspectives, and its meanings may be shared. But before we start, it may be useful to preface some of his common words so that we won't find ourselves without a place to begin.

Aigh: I (pronounced strongly); a place of being - the present and your place within it

Perspective: a position of thought

Stickiness: an impediment or irritant of any kind, physical or mental

(a)/ (to) Wonder: an impulsive effortless movement of thought, brought on by an experience

(to) Listen: solely the act of being presented an idea

(to) Hear: the act of processing into thought or the further contemplation, of what you are presented

Insight of my outlook: the understanding gained from a particular perspective

To view (something) in plane site: to look at the different planes of perspective of an issue; or, to step back and view the idea from many angles

Some-thing: a created thing of this world, be it material, or an idea

No-thing: an understanding of the untrue nature of all "some-things"

Every-thing: an understanding that the true nature of reality is beyond all "some-things"

Sponsoring Notion: a higher ideal, or an idea that stems off and branches into many other perspectives, and their associated behaviors (note: this can be a positive or a negative thing)

Courage of Faith: the will to follow an idea as far as it allows or commitment to your faith (faith being whatever is entertaining the thought, be it a perspective or a sponsoring notion)

Realm: a domain of thought or physical place that has consistent parameters and can be visited, again and again

(to look) in a Mirror: to view yourself or something else through a certain perspective or sponsoring notion

juuju: the innate energy of the universe that engenders and perpetuates every-thing

Whapuuuuuu... Ha...: a slow deep breath, in a steady rhythm

Now that there is groundwork laid in what I hope to be common words, I bid you fond philosophy with one last point: Some may balk at ridiculous phrasings of immaterial things, but to them I say, that with a discerning mind, such exercises in thought can only offer new connections or ways of thinking, and a greater appreciation of familiar ideas, viewed anew.

May I forever take peace in Its liberating dominion.

Joshua Egner

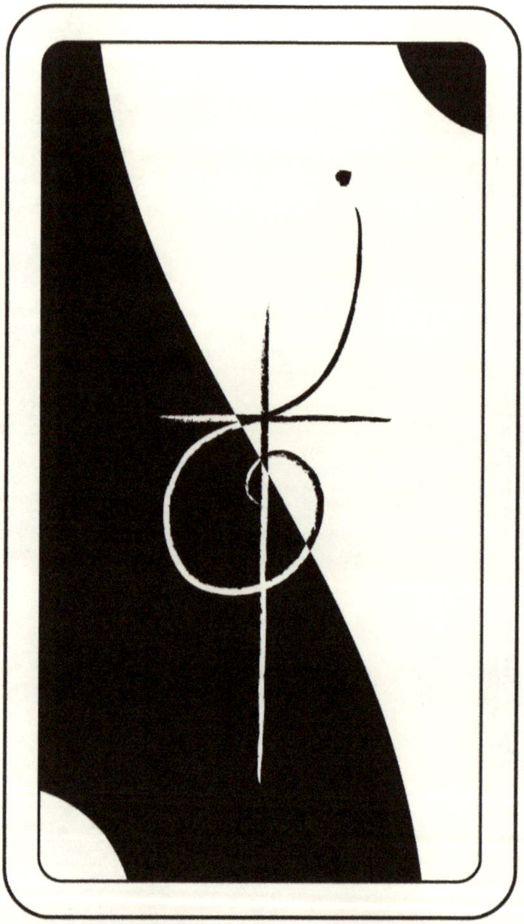

Is This Religious?

Sub-deck: Notions

Is This Religious?

It's not knoing...

The only religion involved in the process is what you bring to your personal work. Whatever your faith is, Aigh want you to hang onto it, you're gonna need it. My sense around religion is that they all have fierce loving compassion, and touch people at their foundations. These readings honor and support those spiritual foundations.

That being said, Aigh do ask that you consider having faith in your faith, so your personal work will be more transformative. Your faith is the foundation for the moral courage needed to learn to be in control, yet choosing not to control, in favor of just being. When the noise of fear arises, Aigh want you to kno your faith has your back. How you come to that faith is up to you.

The journey begins here... the question then becomes:

If we/all of us start at G_od faith and go forward,

how far could we go?

It's not knoing...

the one "thing" ya gotta have to get there - is faith.

Imagine that... and "it" will soon appear.

Peace and Courage to all beings of the realm

Aigh...

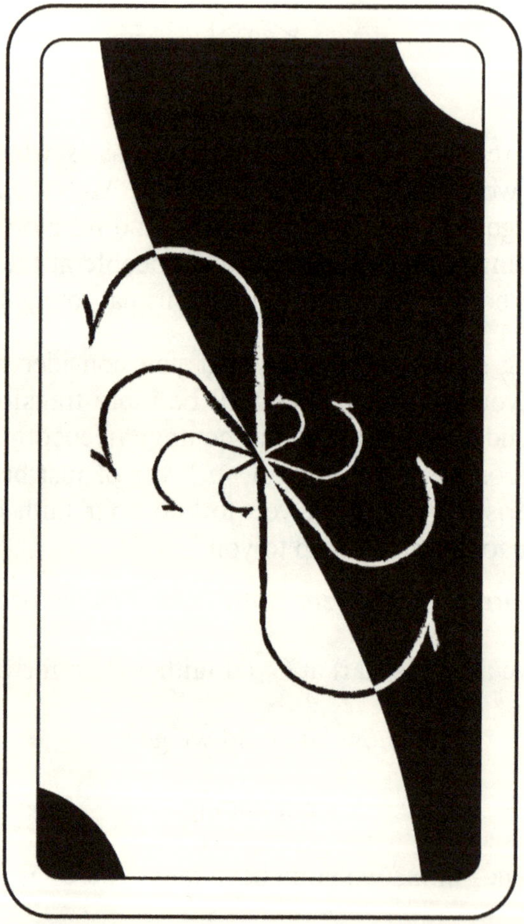

Crazy Buffalo's Reading

Sub-deck: Readings

Crazy Buffalo's Reading

Mirror Cards

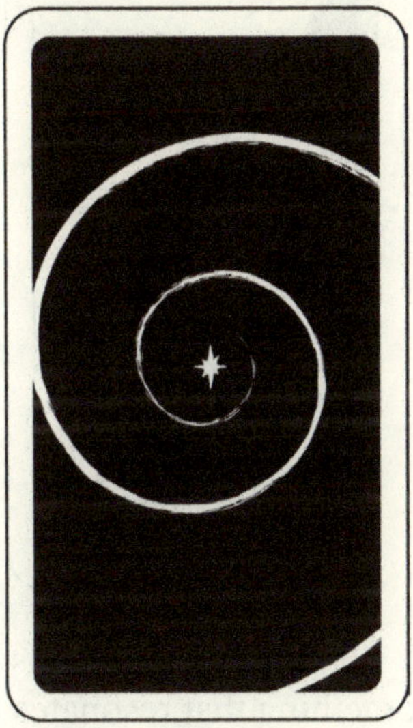

What's to be found here?

G_od faith
a Third Eye's Insight
the chaos of Ego's I
Peace, Love and Joy in the breath of an Everyday Notion
the G_od sense of a Clean Slate

It's not knoing what the next big "thing" is that matters. It's being open enough to hear a common sense resonating in an odd way that just may be crazy enough to spread far beyond what I can think to imagine, after a first reading.

a Third Eye's Insight

Daring to look beyond what I think "I kno" is right, through a Third Eye's Insight, to read something that resonates like no other "thing" in the ever flowing mass of "things" to have crossed my path so far…

These are the Key cards of the realm that may open One to a wonder beyond what Ego's I can think to imagine - truth. G_od faith is the one "thing" that's common in some-thing you may think, no-thing you kno for sure - about the wonder in every-thing One hears, resonating right, in an odd way, to the ear.

Reading aloud to hear the sound of your own voice, breathing in G_od faith with Another, in YinYang, to the judgment typically made in the rush of "things." It's the intuitive "things" in life that causes One to stop-n-catch a breath.

Whapuuuuuu... Ha...

Chaos of Ego's I

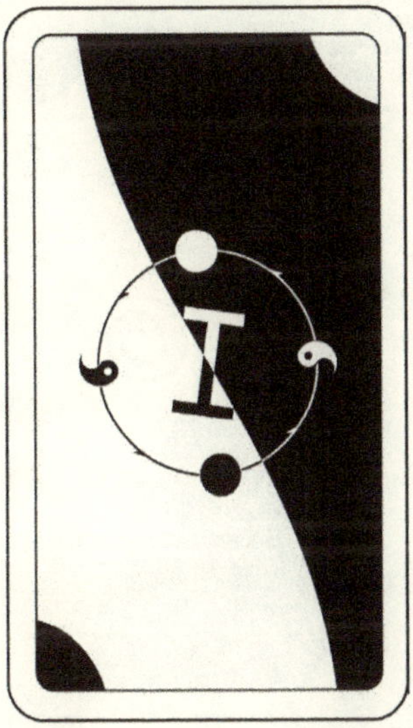

I think "I kno" all about stuff like this when it comes to publishing real bodies of work. Sure... some read this stuff, but the masses... "I don't kno" if they'd get some-thing this WooWoo...

On the other hand, if some-thing like G_od faith were to catch hold, it just may be the next big "thing." And... that means reading "things," like books of cards, decks of cards, etc., seeking a sense of peace to "things," that is hiding in plane sight of what I think "I kno" is out-there.

Imagine that...

So, the question is: What's at risk?

Whapuuuuuu... Ha...

Aigh wonder... and you?

Breath of an Everyday Notion

Whapuuuuuu... Ha... Whapuuuuuu... Ha...

Whapuuuuuu... Ha...

While in the busyness of the stickiness of "what is," three slow deep breaths can alter your perspective of the

"what may be" of "what's next."

And that's not knoing…

The one "thing" ya gotta have to get there - is faith.

Imagine that...

Ha... Whapuuuuuu...

G_od Sense of a Clean Slate

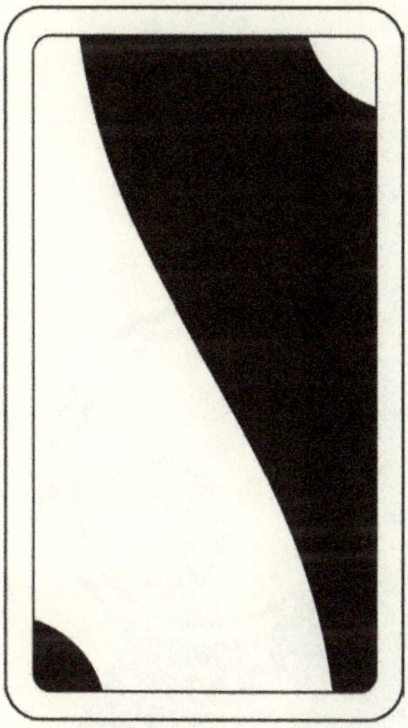

So... What is at risk?

Some-thing you may think, No-thing you kno for sure, missing the next big "thing" because Every-thing I think "I kno" tells me this is non-sense, at first blush.

But... here's the G_od "thing" about taking three slow deep breaths, in the scheme of "things." Aigh'm aware enough to kno any-thing like a hand of G_od faith, when starting with a Clean Slate, is a true G_od sense Aigh should look into.

Seeing a familiar path, Aigh'm free to wonder beyond what I think "I kno" is right... in G_od faith, with a knoing sense of T.S. Eliot's truth, as a journey begins anew.

Peace and Courage to all beings of the realm

Aigh...

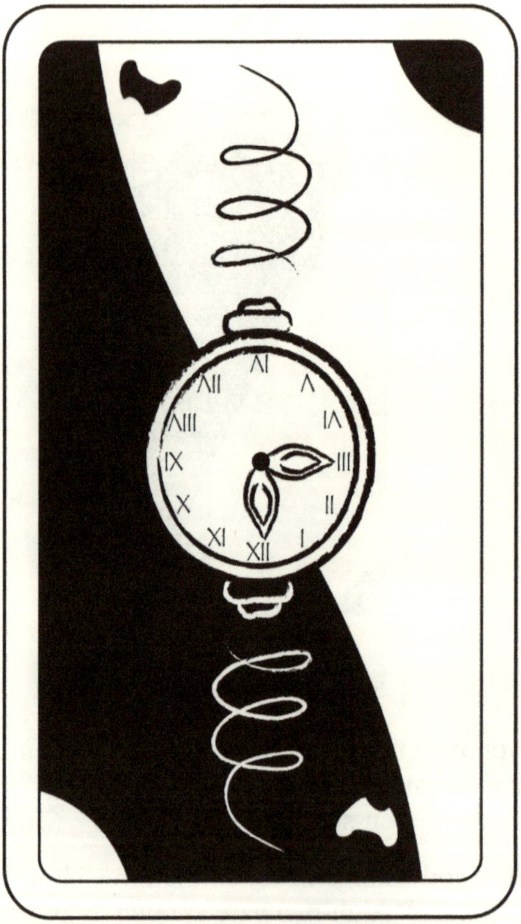

Well, hello Alice...

Sub-deck: Musings

Well, hello Alice...

Whapuuuuuu... Ha...

Alice/Ecila: Hello - Hey! How do you kno my name? And... who are you?

One: Oh... Aigh'm no-One you kno to look at, but you've known a sense of me, since you can remember hearing migh voice. Do you kno where you are?

Alice/Ecila: I think so...

One: Ah... it's no-wonder.

Alice/Ecila: What do you mean by that?!

One: Well... because you think you kno where you are, it's no-wonder you can't see everything that's black and white around you. Your outlook is blinding your insight, trying to think what must be imagined. Do you see now?

Alice/Ecila: "I don't kno," since you color it that way. Nothing seems to make sense this way, it's all opposite from what I thought to be right. How can that be?

One: Aigh see you're dizzy from looking at the extremes. Aigh'm breathing here in the center of things. Join me... won't you?

Whapuuuuuu... Ha... Whapuuuuuu... Ha...

Aigh feel a balance to this place... and you?

Alice/Ecila: "I don't kno" what I feel, but Aigh'm not too afraid to catch my breath. In fact, it feels like there's room to expand here. What... are you doing here?

One: Oh… Aigh was just wondering - what would be at risk if non-sense made sense in an odd way? Personally, Aigh can't think to imagine how different every-thing would be. Aigh'd have to wonder why Aigh hadn't seen it sooner.

So, what's up with you Alice? Did you just arise thinking you're in wonderland? No-wonder you're in the dark as to the way "things" come into balance here. It's migh sense you've been gone since you were born.

Alice/Ecila: You sound as mad as the Hatter in a way only a striped Cheshire can look. "I kno" you. "I kno" I've talked to you, I've been down this road before. Don't you remember me?

One: Yes…. Like Aigh said earlier, it's no-wonder, it's all in your reflection. It takes the courage of G_od faith to look into "it." You'll recall more as you go now.

Alice/Ecila: Go! I just got here! Where am I going?!

One: On your way, it's what's next in the cards for you.

Alice/Ecila: Where do Aigh start? How do Aigh read this stuff? What do Aigh use for a sense of direction?

One: Well, since you're here, this would be the place to start - you might want to mark this spot, it's where "it" all begins. This stuff is meant to be read aloud in G_od faith, it only sounds hard - the fun is in recalling all the voices. Direction… hum… it's not knoing... the route is yours to take, how it comes is by your own hand as you deal the cards for your-self.

Alice/Ecila: How will "I kno" what to do along the way?

One: It's not knoing..., but think of it this way, if you must. "I kno" I've never come to "it" before. Besides "I don't kno" if "it" even exists, given all the texts are ancient on the subject. What's "not knoing" is my sense G_od faith is the one "thing" to see me through times like these. Coming to "kno" "it" that way just makes G_od sense to me." Make sense?

Alice/Ecila: That's all you can tell me? And… the rest I've got to come to on my own?

One: Yes - n - No. Yes in the sense the journey is yours. And… no, you'll only be alone when you choose. Migh voice is ever a breath away, just in case you're in need of someone to speak the words in G_od faith for you.

Alice/Ecila: G_od... so, you're going to be with me then? You kno the way - right?

One: Whapuuuuuu… Ha… Whapuuuuuu… Ha… Whapuuuuuu… Ha...

It's not knoing… the one "thing" ya gotta have to get there - is faith.

Alice/Ecila: Hey! One last "thing!" Is this wonderland?

One: Migh sense: Yes… Migh truth: it's not knoing… Migh being: Whapuuuuuu… Ha…

The choice is yours, dear Alice/Ecila, it's what's next. Imagine that… and "it" will soon appear.

Ha… Whapuuuuuu…

Peace and Courage to all beings of the realm

Aigh...

Dealing with 39 cards…

Sub-deck: Musings

Dealing with 39 cards…

Whapuuuuuu... Ha...

Another: 39 cards... huh? Are you sure we're playing with a full deck? I've played with 52 before, and peered into the Tarot's 78 once or twice, but, 39 - that doesn't sound like enough. And... it kinda feels funny, like it's a little light in my hand.

One: Hum... G_od question, my sense is: Yes - n - No. Yes in the sense that 3 is a wavy sign of faith that when doubled makes 6, which is the mirror reflection of its square - 9. So you see, 39 adds up when you factor the key number. And... no in the sense that there are many more cards to be played, but every-thing and everyone has to start somewhere, and 39 is enough for that.

It's one "thing" to write a bunch of cards, but it's a whole nother "thing" to bring them together with OneAnother to gain insight from their mirrored reflections. And... whether you think it's all doodoo... or wonder at its WooWoo... is not what matters. It's having the G_od sense to wonder in G_od faith, just to satisfy One's own curiosity. It's not knoing... what's next after that, it's in the randomness of the cards you've assembled by hand, with a sense of your own G_od faith.

Whapuuuuuu... Ha...

Ok... every-thing has to start somewhere, so, naturally, stepping into the story would be what's next. Everyone has one, so it's kind of like a shared common "thing" we all have some sense of. Wondering on... it then makes common sense that 4 of the fixed cards in the deck come from the story. And... just so One doesn't lose their way completely, 4 notions to ponder from the scribes hold fixed positions, as well, setting the foundation for a working deck of 12.

Next would be a random array of Wild Eyes that filter “things” in ways One intuitively knos, for some odd reason. Hear... 3 is key when looking into the pool of 9.

The question at this point is: “What’s at risk?”

A sense of my truth: “There’s always some-thing about every-thing at risk and no-thing “I kno” will ever change that or “it” would’ve happened already. So, in a working deck of 12, 3 Wild Eyes should also be considered a fairly common “thing” to look out through. When and/or how often they’ll arise is not knoing... it’s all in the cards One draws. The truth is they keep “things” interesting. Small wonders...

Blindly selecting 3 eyes from the pool, to combine with the eight others, brings the deck to eleven. Set the 6 remaining eyes aside for another time. It’s at this point we add the final “thing” One needs to have in their hand before starting this journey - a breath of fresh air.

Whapuuuuuu... Ha...

This brings us to the realm of the cards. A vast caldron of 21 that the Wild Eyes bring into view, looking to share the insights brought forth in the moment. It’s not knoing... what One may encounter that matters, it’s having the courage of your own G_od faith to look beyond what “I think” is right, to see AnotherOne’s insight that counts. Knoing one “thing” as you shuffle along - all spirits really do choose what to reflect on for themselves... it would be what’s next.

One may see some-thing one time or hear no-thing another, it’s knoing every-thing is drawn by your own hand in G_od faith that matters. It’s no-wonder “I think” it’s gotta be fixed, somehow, otherwise all of this would be for my own G_od sense of “things,” in YinYang, to what “I think” about everything else.

Now “I kno” that sounds crazy when Aigh say it, but if I stop to think about how every-thing else seems to be going nuts these days, anyway, what’s one more “thing” if it helps me catch my breath? Whapuuuuuu... Ha...

Then... if "it" really is not knoing... then "I don't kno" what there is to be afraid of when dealing with 39 cards in G_od faith. And... if a G_od sense fills me as a result, well... that's just a bonus for opening my mind to higher "things."

Another: No-wonder they feel so light in my hand! Aigh'm the One who's dealing all the cards, so, naturally, Aigh'm comfortable hearing myself wondering along, as Aigh read further.

One: Aigh... so, One could say the weight of dealing your own cards lies not in the number in play, but in how One reads the reflections, as they resonate in turn.

Another: Whapuuuuuu... Aigh get "it" now! When dealing with 39 cards, some-thing beyond every-thing "I think I kno is right" is what Aigh'm supposed to be looking for. As for not knoing... well that's the mirror reflection of my own G_od faith - Aigh no longer fear that "I don't kno." And... knoing that really does give me a balanced G_od sense of myself. Ha...

One: Imagine that...

Ha... Whapuuuuuu...

Peace and Courage to all beings of the realm
Aigh...

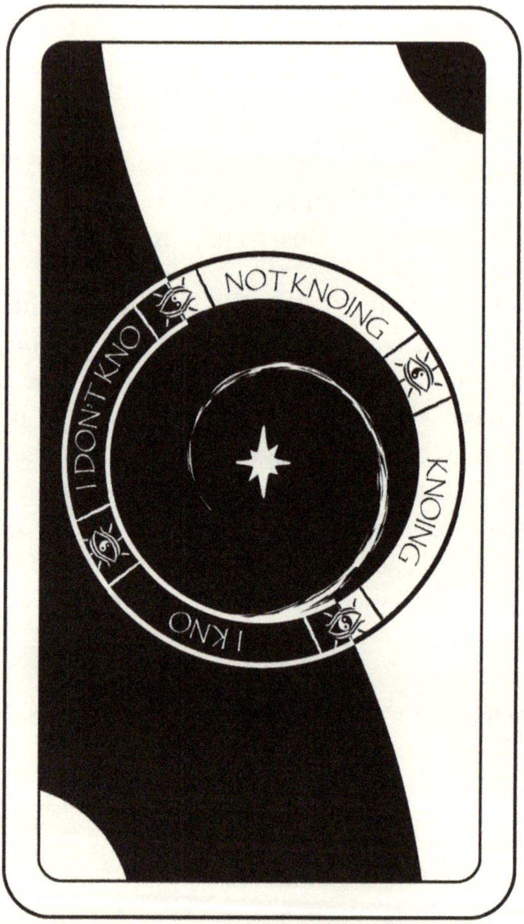

One to Touch Base

Sub-deck: Readings

One to Touch Base

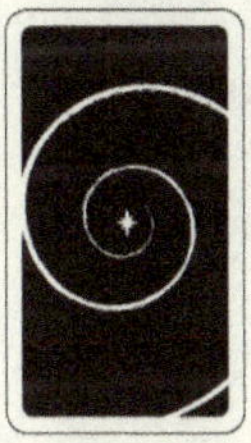

While in the midst of “things”, it’s a G_od “thing” to stop and draw one card, catching the breath of some-thing, which may have no-thing to do with any-thing in particular, but may alter every-thing that’s next – it’s not knoing…

Whapuuuuuu... Ha...

Should some-thing about the one resonate, look to pass “it” along to another, sharing in G_od faith.

But... if you see or hear no-thing, it’s no wonder - you may want to add a couple, making “it” a common reading. At that point, some-thing of another reflection shines a light on every-thing One is meant to hear, insightfully.

And... if every-thing about the one wraps you in G_od faith, then bask in the light glow of G_od sense that follows.

Ha... Whapuuuuuu...

Peace and Courage to all beings of the realm

Aigh…

A Common Reading

Sub-deck: Readings

Three Card Reading

A Common Reading

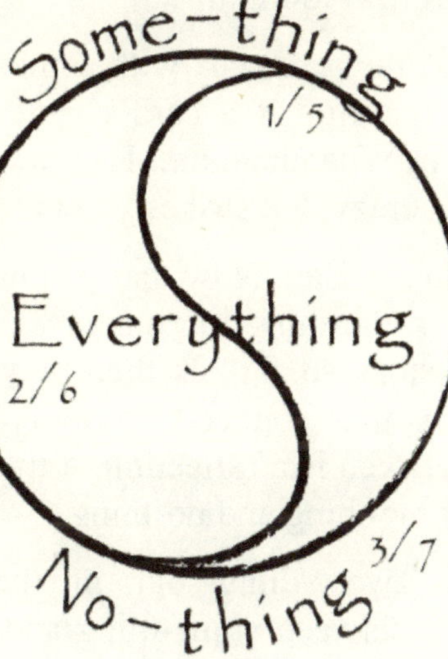

Three is a key number when turning to insight for outlook. With a simple twist, it becomes a wavy sign of G_od faith, forming the mirror image of its multiples. This reading is simple, as far from some-thing as you can get is no-thing, and every-thing in between is a reflection of "what is." Not knoing what to think, it's no wonder some-thing about all this seems familiar, although "I kno" I've never read any-thing quite like this before. No-thing seems to make sense at first glance, yet every-thing resonates in an odd, random way – it's not knoing.

1) Whether you come to this place with "no-thing" in hand, or are beginning your journey here, shuffle, then select some-thing for your-self, and place it somewhere.

2) Next, draw on no-thing in particular and place it far from some-thing. If you have no-thing in hand, now would be the time to set it down, as well.

3) Now, look to the "things" that are left, and choose a glimpse of every-thing, now that some-thing and no-thing are on the table.

4) Any drawn card can be randomly rotated 180 degrees, one time, after all of the cards have been drawn. Listen to hear your own intuitive G_od sense of "things," when pondering such moves in G_od faith.

5) It's a G_od thing to start with something that catches your eye. Ever mindful of a card's patterns, One takes a slow deep breath, Whapuuuuuu... Ha... and looks for some-thing that sounds crazy, but strikes you in a funny way.

6) Whapuuuuuu... Ha... Now that you have some-thing to hold onto, look at no-thing in your hand. How does the pattern shade the story so far? Is there any-thing where no-thing was before, that connects to some-thing, because every-thing in between is a reflection of the evolution of "things," between some-thing and no-thing?

7) So... with every-thing out in the open now, caught somewhere between some-thing and no-thing, it's time to see every-thing for what "it" is. Whapuuuuuu... Ha... It's not knoing where every-thing is that's important, it's having the courage of G_od faith to look deeper for connections, when the picture looks like non-sense, in the moment. It is here that One may choose to look Insightout of Infinities Loop for another reflection. But if some-thing about every-thing sounds like enough for now, be sure no-thing is left untouched, as you let go of "things" in order to sit with "it" for a while.

In the middle of every-thing going on, there's always some-thing coming up that's no-thing expected, that changes the way "it" goes. It's not knoing how one "thing" can alter every-thing that matters, "it's" knoing G_od faith is some-thing that will see any One through any-thing, even if no-thing seems right in the moment. The G_od sense that comes from a common reading, is every-thing One will need, to get past the extremes of all these "things" insight of what you wonder about all this.

Imagine that...

Peace and Courage to all beings of the realm

Aigh…

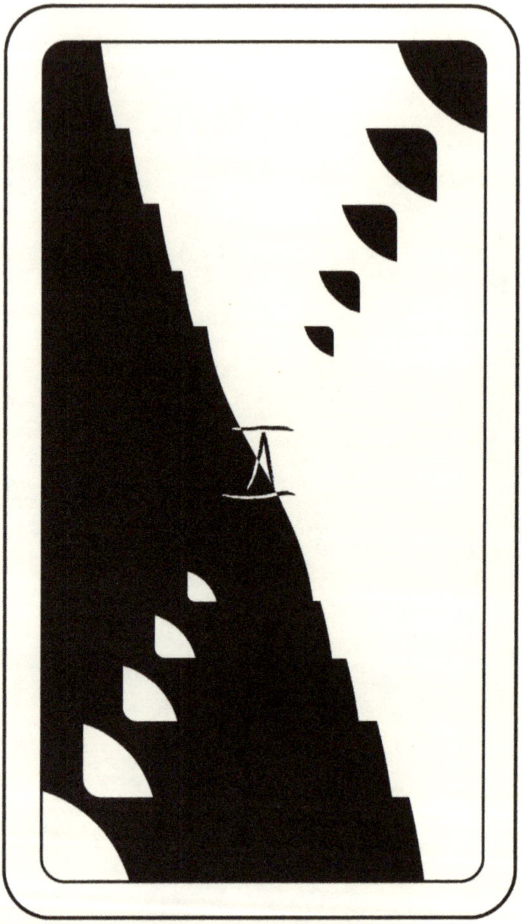

Insightout of Infinity's loop

Sub-deck: Readings

Five Card Reading

Insightout of Infinity's loop

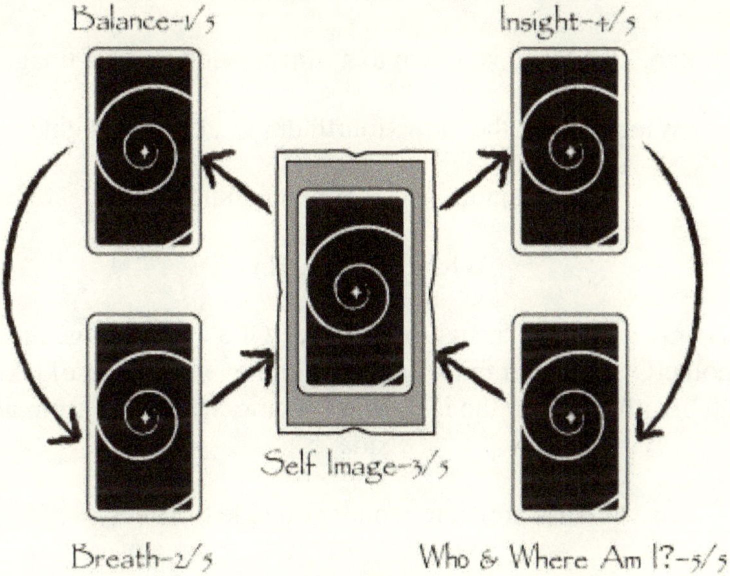

Order of Reading

Shuffle and cut the deck until it feels "right", being mindful of this time. Cards to remain face down until all are drawn.

Any drawn card can be randomly rotated 180 degrees, one time, after all of the cards in the reading have been drawn. Listen to hear your own intuitive G_od sense of "things" when pondering such moves in G_od faith.

Each card is read side-to-side to determine Masculine / Feminine orientation, as well as top & bottom, to establish light & shadow positioning.

Cards are to be turned over and read in the following order:

(taking a slow deep breath)

Whapuuuuuu... Ha...

Tentatively, the first card is drawn into a place of Balance -

Quickly, a second Breath is drawn…

Whapuuuuuu... Ha... Whapuuuuuu... Ha...

"I kno," the third, is drawn to a mirror, seeking Self Image;

Winded from the blow, fourth draws akin to Insight.

Whapuuuuuu... Ha... Whapuuuuuu... Ha...

Whapuuuuuu... Ha...

Fifth draws wonder "insightout," to see One's Self Image through AnotherOne's G_od faith, balanced in the G_od sense of taking enough breaths, to hear the insights of seeing Self Image from another side.

What's at risk to wonder outside the lines?

It's not knoing...

Imagine that... and you will kno "enough" to look within.

Ha... Whapuuuuuu...

Peace and Courage to all beings of the realm

Aigh…

Journaling Page

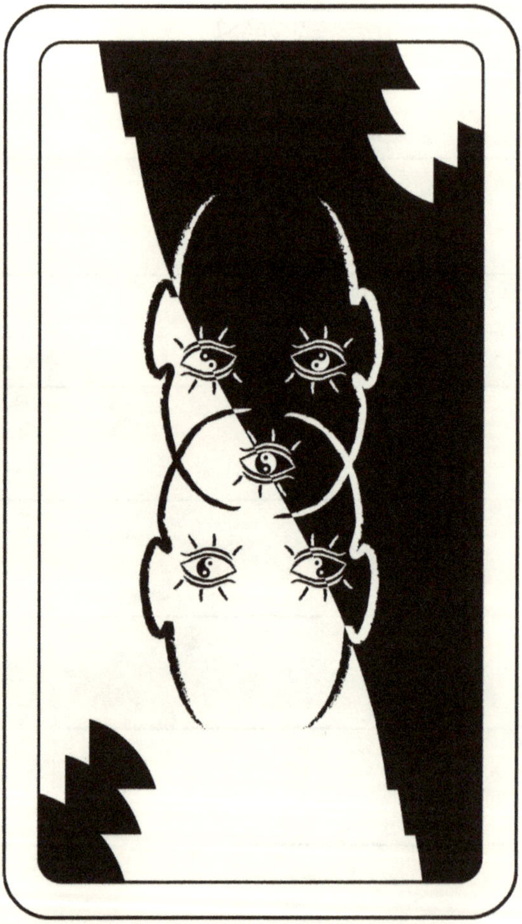

Wild Eye Reading

Sub-deck: Readings

Wild Eye Reading

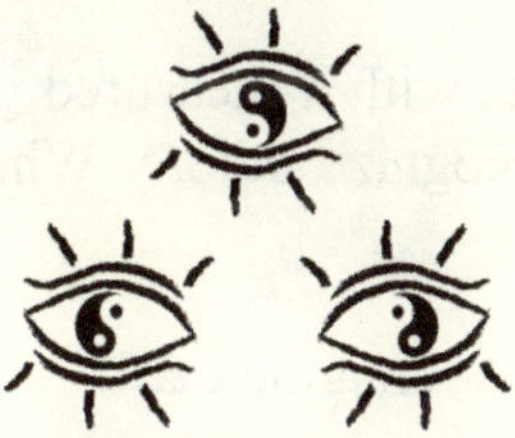

Daring to look insightout is a courageous “thing.”

Coming to an understanding of what is being looked at starts with knoing which eyes are being used to gain focus. Wild Eye Reading is just the “thing” to triangulate random points, to gain insight from outside the box of “I kno.”

“It” all starts by summoning the Wild Eyes of the deck to come together, bringing all eyes to attunement. Shuffle, then spread the Eyes face down.

With One’s right eye closed, choose with your left; now, it’s no-wonder in mirror reflection, “I think I kno” which one “it” is, so, choose “it,” and place “it” in the right spot.

With One’s left eye closed, seek with the right intention, daring to wonder which one “it” is, placing “it” left of the right one.

Now all that remains is to close both the left and the right, so the inner “Aigh” can select its lens of choice, placing it in the Third Eye’s position.

From this place, start with the right, then go straight to the left, seeking the extremes.

At this point, use the power of the one in the middle to find a balanced connection, honing One's inner sight.

Looking insightout from this place of free breath, bask for a moment, fearless of all the "things" this brings to mind.

Whapuuuuuu… Ha… Whapuuuuuu… Ha…

Whapuuuuuu… Ha…

Here in this distant space, with a measured glance, One is free to see what was too close to recognize before. What's next is not knoing… that's for you to choose.

Imagine that…

Peace and Courage to all beings of the realm

Aigh…

Journaling Page

Crystal Healing for the Third-Eye Chakra

Sub-deck: Healings

Crystal Healing for the Third-Eye Chakra

Amethyst is a divine gem of content spiritual vibrations. Honing the Tao sign, the Aigh basks in the invigorating strength of peaceful stability that a starling experiences just before birth. The calm, soothing juuju of this stone channels the free breath of common sense to the Third Eye's perception. Vibrates: number 3

Azurite is the stone of the heavens, allowing the Third Eye to see with clarity, along with the ability to speak of its endeavors. Induces ethereal links - clearing the mind of doubt and worry, freeing it to push beyond stickiness. From here, creativity is improved; seeing from a heart's place, it kindles compassionate, loving sense to what One thinks. Vibrates: number 1

Charoite is the light of brotherhood, shining from the Aigh to all in its realm. Ever a rock for attention, it allows the mind's Eye to see the open door in the shadow of the passage's end. We end at the start – it's what's next. Attuned to a knoing sense of being, it brings forth the ultimate benefits of the Third Eye's second sight. Vibrates: number 7

Kyanite is akin to Citrine in that neither stone collects nor retains the Shadow King's dark intentions. This gem aligns the chakras in an instant with the conscious intention of the holder. One of the best stones for attunement, its energy has limitless sight of its use. With its tranquil juuju, Kyanite is one of Buddha's favorite sedentary rocks of insight. Vibrates: number 4

Lapis is the rock of the origin. In the Aigh's presence of the One, the mysteries of a not knoing notion of faith, that a Yang's act guided by a Yin's intuitive sense, is the unity needed to see the image in the mirror of what's next. Shining the light of clarity in the dark realm, Lapis aids in the release of the dark story of "what was", to bask in the One's knoing radiance of "what is." Vibrates: number 3

Sodalite is a stone of commonality of purpose in the fellowship of solidarity within a group. Ever the vigilant Aigh, it sees the One's knoing sense of self trust, leading to trust in others, with a mutual dependence on the free breath, seeing the truth in the mirror. Vibrates: number 4

Sugilite juuju carries the One's gentle loving message to mind, bringing the holder the free breath of peace, releasing the constriction of breathlessness. While in the breath of sedentary silence, the Aigh senses with inspiring confidence the state of being "on top" of its realm manifests. Vibrates: numbers 2, 3 & 7

Chanting Breath of Activation

Lying prone on your back, place stones at or slightly above the eyebrows' center mass, ensuring all beings are connected. With the intention of each crystal's sponsoring notion of wonder present - free your mind of everything, to allow some-thing to open to no-thing it has ever received before. Chanting the vibrational numbers of each gem, in the peaceful silence of free breath, activates this earthly healing.

Duration: 5 to 10 minutes, repeat chant three to five times with slow… deep breaths, envisioning the freedom from blockages that you experience, with the breath of your intention between.

Whapuuuuuu… Ha… Whapuuuuuu… Ha…

Whapuuuuuu… Ha…

Oneee… Whapuuuuuu… Ha…

Twoooo… Twoooo… Whapuuuuuu… Ha…

Threeee… Threeee… Threeee… Whapuuuuuu… Ha…

Fourrrr… Fourrrr… Fourrrr… Fourrrr… Whapuuuuuu… Ha…

Sevennn… Sevennn… (said 7 times) Whapuuuuuu… Ha…

Ha… Whapuuuuuu…

Peace and Courage to all beings of the realm

Aigh…

Illusion #1:

Is the need to be religiously "right" worth killing over?

Sub-deck: Illusions

Illusion #1

Is the need to be religiously "right" worth killing over?

It's not knoing…

Aigh am not a religious being of the realm, nor have Aigh studied the religions of it. Aigh have chosen to have faith in migh faith, faith in the manifestation of migh destiny, and faith in the One all-"knoing" Spirit.

Aigh honor those who choose to accept religious faith and stand in the light of written lore. Migh sense is that all religions believe in the same universal being. Ever the master of personas, "it's" known by the many images of the myth of "its" label. My belief is that every spirit chooses, either consciously or unconsciously, whether to have faith in its own faith, or faith in a chronicle written by others.

The Zealots spin the yarn preaching the Shadow King's medicine of "being right." Lines of "I kno" are drawn, leading to the disconnection and Trust No One of the King's intention. Countless G_od Souls have marched to surrender, chanting the King's mantra: "I kno, I'm right." The blind crusaders march forth across the sands of time, while the Dark Shadows of little men siphon off the spoils from the martyr's Jihad in the realm. All the while, the souls of the TwinTowers rest in ever lasting peace, for they are not the Ones suffering from the loss.

Living in the light of "I don't kno," the Shadow Kings and their minions are lost - "not knoing…" if their spirits can breathe the Peace, Love and Joy offered by the Blind I's of the realm. They fear the sense that an existence based on acceptance, without ownership, of another's faith, would be the ascension foretold in the text of their own accounts.

Wrapped in their self-judgments, they taste the bitter bile of their own hateful medicine.

The G_od Souls of the realm continue the struggle to manifest Peace, in hope the spirits of the combatants sense the juuju… in the coming winds, leading to the silencing of arms, while the moon cycles well beyond the Mayans' sense of time.

What's next after that is not knoing… one "thing" for sure is: if all the stories are religiously true, most of us will pass on through, quite naturally, once again. The others will end up wading in the vast, hot crude of their desire – dying to expire.

In the light of silent breath, all beings of the realm stand before their God to hear the message of "what's next". The war for control of the realm is the never-ending folly; ascension to Peace need only come once in the human lifetime.

What's at risk?

Something – Nothing – Everything

It's not knoing…

the one "thing" ya gotta have to get there - is faith.

Imagine that… and "it" will soon appear.

Peace and Courage to all beings of the realm

Aigh…

Journaling Page

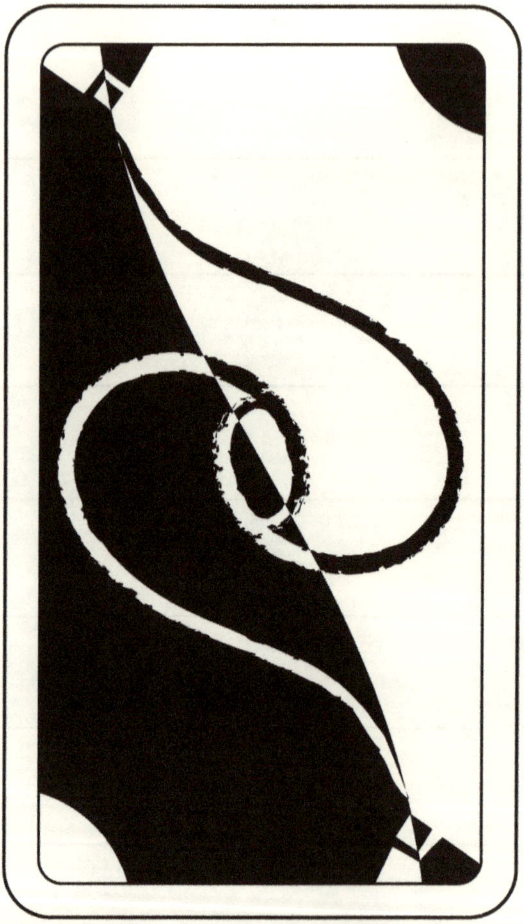

No-thing of Value

Sub-deck: Story

No-thing of Value

One: Whapuuuuuu… Ha…

Another: Ya kno what?! I've read enough of this stuff to kno, it makes no sense that "I kno" of! And… there's no-thing of value to be found that I can see.

One: Finally… we've come to no-thing of value between us.

Another: So… what do you mean by that?

One: Oh, Aigh'm One who knos some-thing about no-thing, that is more valuable than any-thing that Ego's I can think to imagine.

Another: Really?! Well... this I gotta hear.

One: Ok, this should be fun… Hmm… well, here we are with no-thing of value between us, mirror images of OneAnother in that respect. Wondering on, the "thing" that we share, that some-thing in common is no-thing of value as it stands.

Another: Now you're scaring me…

One: You'll be fine, just take a deep breath.

Another: Whapuuuuuu… Ha...

One: Now… where Aigh come from, that means that neither of us has any-thing to lose, because we each have no-thing of value binding us. From here, as One sees their reflection in AnotherOne's eyes, they become One with each other, with no-thing between them but the sound of their flushed breaths.

Whapuuuuuu… Ha… Whapuuuuuu… Ha…

Another: See!!! I knew it! Here you go again, making some-thing out of no-thing!

One: Oh, Aigh don't claim to kno no-thing; Aigh can just tell you a whole lot about it, it's what's next.

Another: Well... at least that's some-thing that sounds true. Ok, so what would you kno about some-thing if you have no-thing of value to say?

One: Hmm… it's not knoing. But if Aigh did kno, Aigh'd say it's somewhere between every-thing and no-thing. And… knoing that one "thing" gives me the courage to seek a G_od faith balance between the extremes. And the peace of free breath that emanates from this is truly some-thing to come to - truth.

Another: Why does every-thing you say sound like talking circles? I'll admit "I don't kno" any-thing, much less some-thing about no-thing. I'm afraid this all sounds like a leap of faith to me.

One: Exactly… you do see!

Another: See?!! Ok… I surrender, peace already - I'm dying here! What do I see?

One: Whapuuuuuu… Ha… Whapuuuuuu… Ha… Whapuuuuuu… Ha…

You see it takes a leap of faith to find the courage required to live beyond what feels like it's going to kill you. And… since we've got no-thing of value between us, neither One of us has a "thing" to lose, when G_od faith is the only "thing" we share in common.

Another: Well... I gotta hand it to you. You really do kno no-thing! And... you're right it takes a leap of faith to get through this stuff, and if that's the "G_od thing" between us you keep talking about, then... I guess... I see... since you put it that way. Why was it so hard to come to this point?

One: What do you mean!? We started with no-thing of value as some-thing in common. Every-thing that followed was a journey we took together that ended with you seeing a G_od thing between us. Talk about popping from one extreme to another, kinda makes me wonder… and you?

Another: Truly, I can't think to imagine how you come up with this stuff.

One: It's no-wonder - really. Imagine that…

Ha… Whapuuuuuu…

Peace and Courage to all beings of the realm

Aigh...

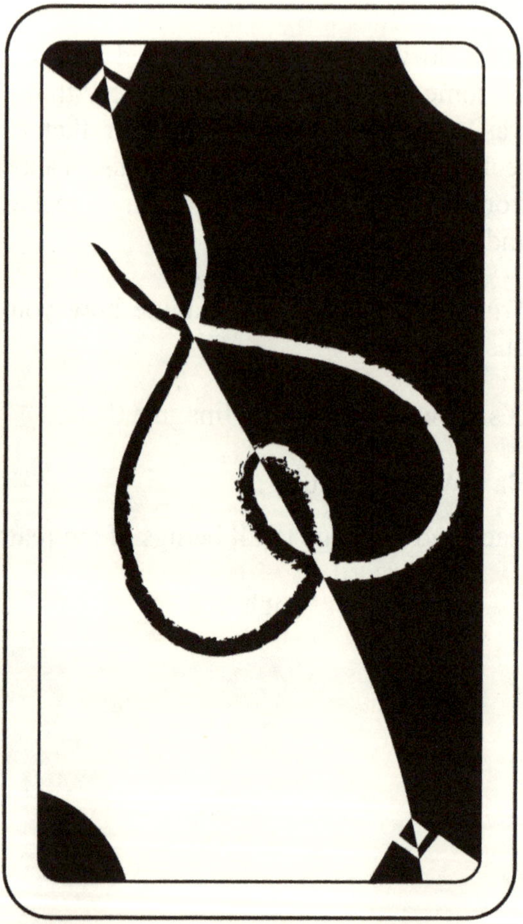

Some-thing of Value

Sub-deck: Story

Some-thing of Value

One: Whapuuuuuu… Ha…

Another: Hey! Now wait a minute! You can't just make some-thing out of no-thing and leave it at that, that's not fighting fair! It's not my fault this all sounds so foreign to me, I don't ever recall hearing "things" spoken this way before!

One: Whapuuuuuu… Ha… Whapuuuuuu… Ha…

Another: Well…?@! What does G_od faith get me now that Aigh've seen "it?"

One: Hmm… it's not knoing… Who are you fighting? Aigh'm mirrorly reflecting on what you were saying. The G_od "thing" you saw was a reflection of your own G_od faith. It seems this has unsettled you for some reason.

Another: Some reason?! Are you KIDDING ME! Aigh just saw a G_od thing! I told you "I'm afraid this all sounds like a leap of faith to me." And… off you go on one of your monologues, stirring every-thing up, till it's not knoing to me which "thing" you're talking about. And… the next thing "I kno," I feel a G_od sense come between us. How does that happen?@!

One: Truth?

Another: Naturally…!

One: It's not knoing… "It" may all sound crazy at first, but awakening to this is much easier than it sounds, after One first catches a clear breath of "it" for themselves.

Another: Whapuuuuuu… It wasn't so easy for me. Ha… How do you explain that?

One: Stickiness…

Another: See… this is how you do it - you just changed the subject.

One: They're connected. Hanging on to what you think, in fear of seeing some-thing else is akin to stickiness. Getting you to let go took all the "things" Aigh could gather up in the moment. The fact that we started with no-thing of value mirrorly left one "thing" between us. So, seeing G_od faith when it's the only "thing" there is easy. And… it's enough of a G_od thing to end on that note.

Another: End?@! What are you talking about? If this is some-thing of value, then Aigh want to hang onto it for dear life! What happened to every-thing between? This is all too heady to stay here for long.

One: It's not knoing… but it's all there. It takes the courage of One's faith to seek a place of balance, when reflecting on every-thing between. It's all in the cards, dealing with them will lead One to see many insights. How it alters your outlook is for you to choose.

Another: So... you're saying, Aigh'm supposed to have faith in the cards then - right?

One: It's not knoing… but if One sees some-thing arise from no-thing, then every-thing that follows just may be a wonder to behold. The wonder of "it" is - you can't think to imagine "it" - truth.

Another: Hmm… So, if Aigh have the courage to follow along in G_od faith, at some point before “it” ends, Aigh’ll see the light - right?

One: My sense: Yes… My truth: it’s not knoing… My being: Whapuuuuuu… Ha…

Another: There may be some-thing of value to this yet! Aigh feel all flushed as if warmed by a flame within me. OMG!

One: Yes… Imagine that...

Ha… Whapuuuuuu…

Peace and Courage to all beings of the realm

Aigh...

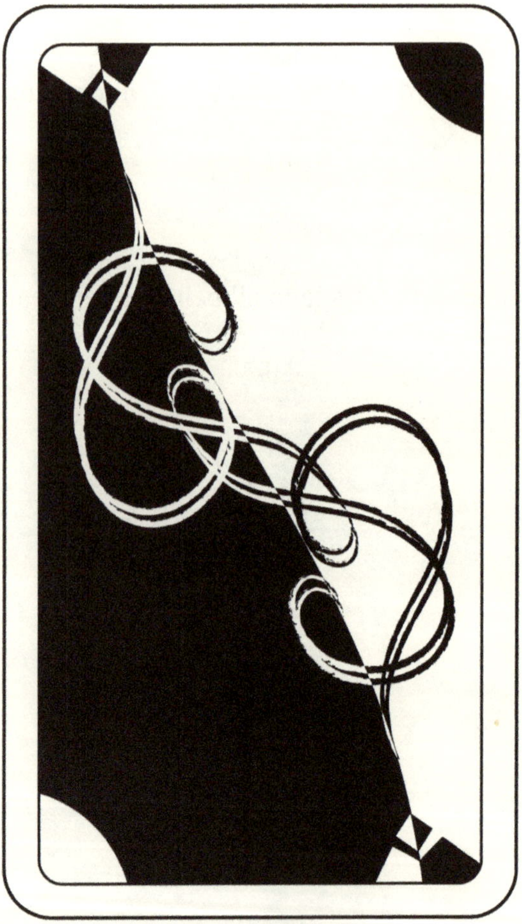

Every-thing Between

Sub-deck: Story

Every-thing Between

One: Whapuuuuuu… Ha…

Another: What did you do to me? Aigh feel all fired up!

One: It's not knoing… but you look all aglow, no-wonder you feel different.

Another: Am Aigh all right? What's happening to me?

One: You're lit, it's but a common thing in YinYang. This is no-thing to fear, some-thing like this is as natural as birthing. You're in G_od company hear.

Whapuuuuuu… Ha… Whapuuuuuu… Ha…

Another: Aigh'm worried about every-thing between, it seems all a blur from here.

One: Does it appear in the past for you?

Another: Yes, looking back, I'm afraid "I don't kno" how I made it from there to here.

One: It's not knoing… what matters is that you've passed on from there to here. And… since it appears behind you, One must find the courage of faith to let go of the story of "it" - so "it" passes away. Make sense?

Another: No! Not at all! Aigh'm just supposed to forget "it" ever happened?

One: Forget… no. One is meant to recall the lessons learned without reliving the trials of the journey. It's enough to kno the outcome from the other side of living through it. Letting go of the rest of "it" is the relief felt in a spark of renewed life.

Another: So, let me see if Aigh've got this: the story is behind me now. And… without that lingering in front of me, Aigh feel that looking forward is some-thing really ahead of me. OMG! What do I do now?

One: It's not knoing… just take "it" as "it" comes - one breath at a time, as the cards are dealt by your own hand, in turn.

Whapuuuuuu… Ha… Whapuuuuuu… Ha…
Whapuuuuuu… Ha…

Life - juuju is one of those "things" that flows to and from you. G_od faith is the "thing" that allows it to resonate from the heart of all "things," lighting the way.

Another: OMG! Aigh can't believe how different every-thing feels from this place. This is too G_od to last - I'm afraid this will pass, as well. How do I hang on to some-thing like this?

One: It's not knoing… but when One sees no-thing of value, kno some-thing of value is at the other extreme. Every-thing between balances on One's G_od faith, it's the one "thing" that will always see you through, when blinded by every-thing rushing at you, all at once.

Another: Aigh see, G_od faith is the eternal flame inside me. And... knoing that one "thing" gives me the strength to look forward on my own, fearless of what "I don't kno" about what's ahead of me. It's a G_od "thing" Aigh'm not alone in this.

One: Yes… Imagine that...

Ha… Whapuuuuuu…

Peace and Courage to all beings of the realm

Aigh…

Journaling Page

Yin Meditation

Sub-deck: Meditations

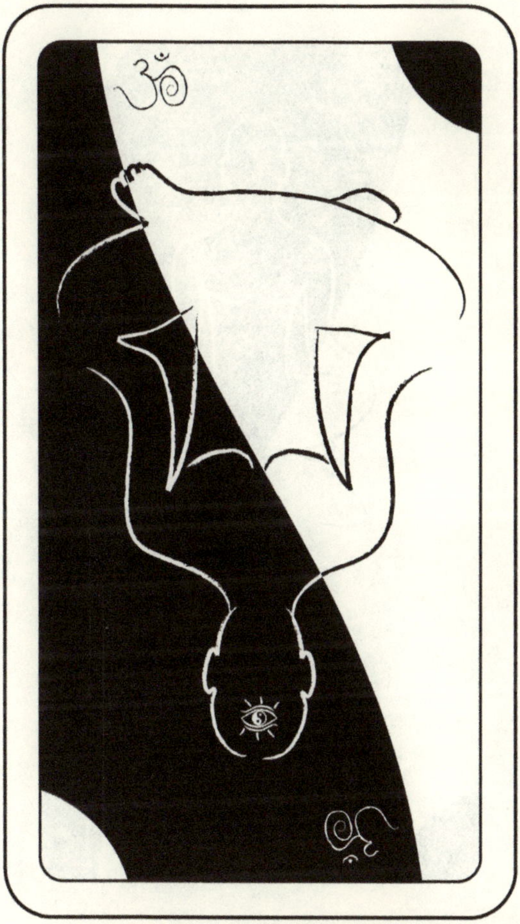

Yang Meditation

Sub-deck: Meditations

Yin Yang Meditation

Sub-deck: Meditations

Breathing Meditations

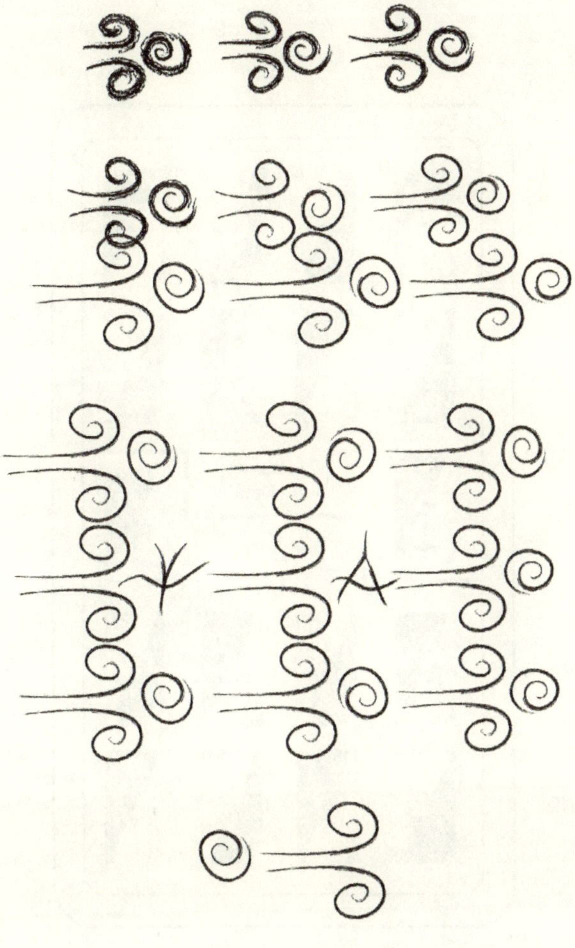

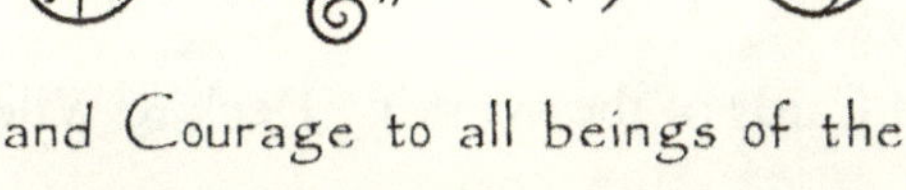

Peace and Courage to all beings of the realm

Cheat Sheet

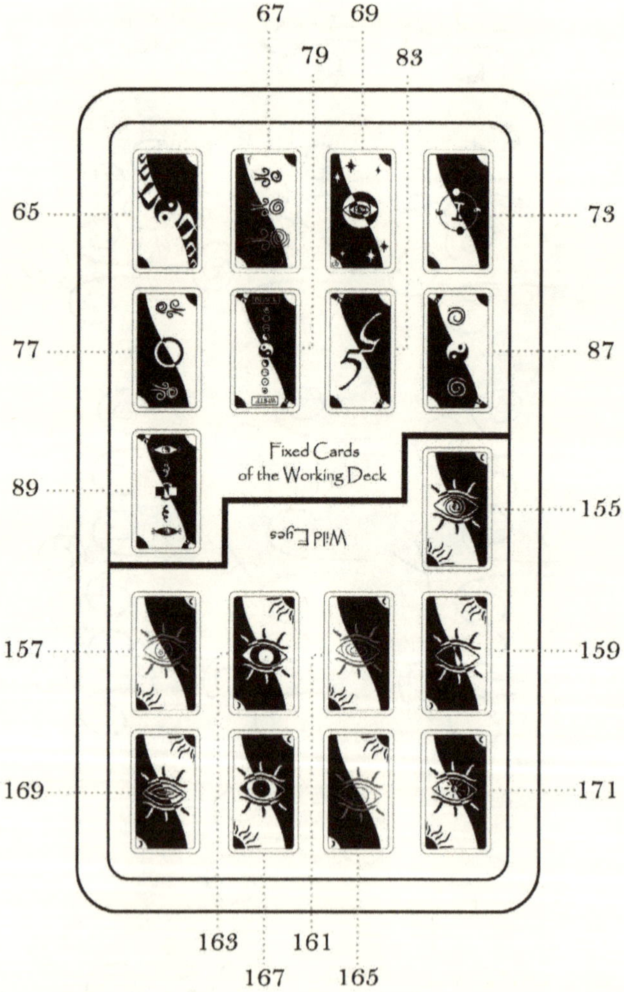

Fixed Cards of the Working Deck & Wild Eyes

Cheat Sheet

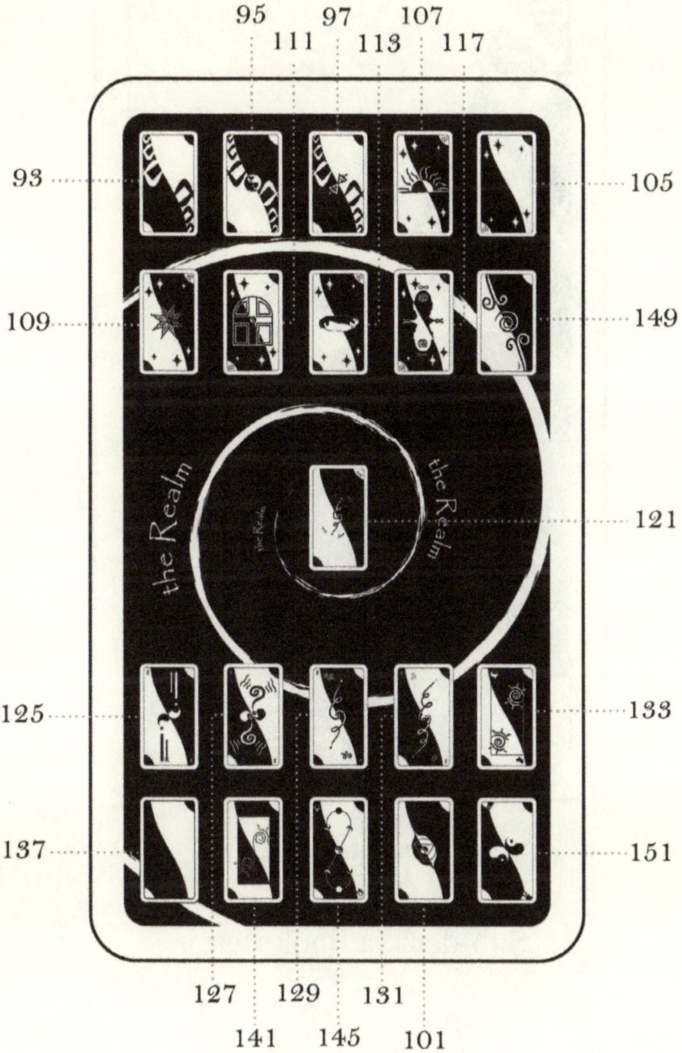

The Realm

Yin-Yang

Sub-deck: a Book that is

Yin-Yang

I am here to mention the impossible necessity, the One that is All, the singularity in which all paradoxes are resolved. Impossible as in lacking the aspect of possibility, making It necessary where everything **is**. A critic may now claim that such a thing is only reason, transcending its sanctioned realm of my mind, but that is far from the truth. It is what men have sought over the millennia, an eternal object, an indubitable belief, a rock upon which to build One's home, and more (in fact all). For such is the masterful Tao and the singular God; It supports all in Its continuous mesh, and breathes all from Its own nature. It is, and always has been, and always will be, for without It, there is no being. Being was first applied to It, and if all shall pass, It will be the last that being applies to. I take joy in the fact that all I can experience is It, and that I cannot **be** without It.

May I forever take peace in Its liberating dominion.

Breath of an Everyday Notion

Sub-deck: Breaths

Breath of an Everyday Notion

Whapuuuuuu… Ha… Whapuuuuuu… Ha…

Whapuuuuuu… Ha…

While in the busyness of the stickiness of "what is," three slow deep breaths can alter your perspective of the

"what may be" of "what's next."

And that's not knoing…

The one "thing" ya gotta have to get there - is faith.

Imagine that…

Ha... Whapuuuuuu...

Peace and Courage to all beings of the realm

Aigh...

Knowing the Future Exists

Sub-deck: Cosmic Herald

Knowing the Future Exists

In the beginning of this vast cosmos, there was but a single point of energy, so singular in fact that it took up no space at all, and from this One point exploded forth all matter and energy that ever was or ever will be. And it is in this One point of energy, radiating out, that a force was imparted onto all matter. This One force, this One moment of being, is what all things in this unknowingly massive universe have in common.

This One energetic burst put gas and dust in motion, it was dark at first, cold and sterile, but soon heat from these moving particles gathered, and compacted and swirled into small points of light, always growing ever brighter and larger. A star was born, and as such so were small, rocky bodies in orbit around the star, small islands in the vast open space where elements could, in their gravitational course, be marooned, where ice came into contact with heat, and water was formed, giving birth to the divine spark of life.

This life was small, a single cell, knowing only what to do because of the forces imparted in its creation. In time, it grew into conscious beings, aware of their own world and their own existence to the degree that they could ponder it. They did ponder free will, the ability of one to enact its will, its cognition in a tangible form.

Then the idea of time, the first barrier created to shield their eyes from the grandeur of existence, all that was is gone, and all that will be is not to be known, and all that is is ever changing. A barrier.

For all that was is light, ever moving, never dying, existence in short. All that is is all that will be and all that will be is simply a matter of knowing. For all that will be is determined only by the forces in the universe, gravity instilling velocity, from there is born friction, the relationship of all matter, from friction is heat, all transformations of the origin of One release.

With the same energy source, nothing in this universe is not tied to that One moment of cosmic being, that One big bang, and so nothing in this universe can alter the course of that One moment of energetic radiance. All things are that One moment, and all that will be is simply a matter of knowing this One truth, for all that will be already is, for it is still tied to that One moment.

The stars rotate only because of that moment, the matter that forms around them does so only by the laws and force imparted in that moment, and so life is born, and guided, by only the force and law imparted in that One moment.

Free will is free only in the sense that it is the product of our consciousness, but our consciousness is the product of forces that can not be altered, so free will, in and of itself, is premeditated to the highest order, and there is nothing in this universe that could change what our will would be simply because of the singularity of all matter and energy.

And there is nothing in the universe that can change the course of this energy, so the future does indeed exist, for it is defined just as the present, and the past, by that, our One moment of cosmic singularity.

Peace

Journaling Page

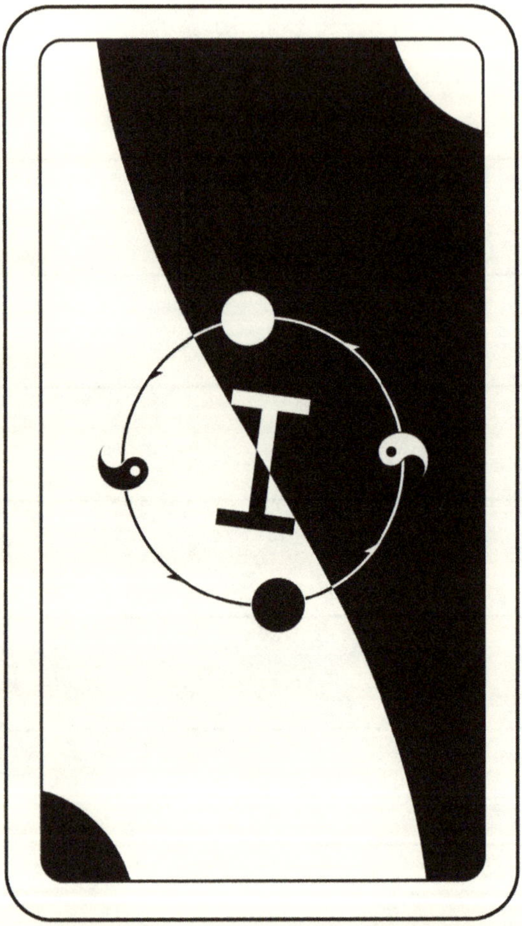

Chaos of Ego's I

Sub-deck: Notions

Chaos of Ego's I

Whapuuuuuu… Ha…

In the middle of everything, there is nothing that escapes something of scrutiny from the chaos of Ego's I. The shadowed image of its gray matter, forever influencing the thoughts of a being's acts of Reason and Impulse.

"I kno" something about everything, and nothing you can say is more than I can think. Wonder is something of a fairy tale, where everything is rosy and nothing is beyond imagination, except a common sense. Whapuuuuuu…

Aigh've listened to everything and see nothing that's real, but Aigh'm unsettled by something Aigh can't put migh finger on. "I don't kno" what it is, nothing's changed, but something is weird about everything lately, and Aigh'm at a loss for breath. Aigh was fine until something happened, causing everything to tighten, and now nothing is on migh mind but the pain in migh chest. With everything flashing before migh eyes, nothing Aigh have ever endured can compare with something like this, as Aigh abruptly surrender to not knoing what's next. Ha…

Alive, and gasping for breath, it's not knoing, the wonder of everything that is transforming, but something of a calming cadence of breathing, that's nothing Aigh'm used to, is coming over me. Whapuuuuuu… Ha…

"I kno" something is up but "I don't kno" what it is. Everything is coming into focus and nothing is different but migh mirror reflection. I think Aigh'd better hide before someone starts wondering what's going on, because Aigh let something slip, followed by a weakening denial that nothing is wrong, in a deep breath that everything is all right – Whapuuuuuu… I think.

With righteous indignation hearing nothing of it, Ego's brain calls everything crazy that is something that's "not knoing" to it. Only the will of faith's courage in One's Heart can muffle Ego's cries of

"I kno, everything will be ruined if something of this non-sense is ingested, leaving nothing but a common sense to be heard.

Torn between clutching for "what was" and accepting "what is," Ego's mind thinks it's going insane with the insight of wonder, awakening to a different sense of being. "'I kno this can't be happening to me, Aigh'm too smart to be taken in by all this non-sense about what was, what is, and not knoing what may be. Aigh'm in control, Aigh just need a moment to breathe so Aigh can collect myself. Whapuuuuuu... Ha...

What's real is that I'm afraid that something has happened, and nothing I can think of will make everything like it was, leaving me vulnerable and powerless. "I don't kno" what I ever did to deserve this, but I'm going to battle this with everything I have, while Aigh search for something of an answer, for why nothing is the same.

I've researched everything, thinking something is out there, and found nothing to loosen this strangle hold on me. Exhausted and out of breath, Aigh'm alone with only One's heartbeat to console me. In a breath of fierce, loving compassion, Aigh stop resisting migh journey, through the fear of what Aigh think, to collapse, wondering what's next. Ha... Whapuuuuuu...

With nothing left but the faith Aigh thought Aigh'd never need, Aigh slowly inhale some-thing, not knoing what it is, as a last ditch effort to connect with every-thing. Having survived a breath of "not knoing," Aigh realize the smothering grip of fear is some-thing that Aigh'm not hanging onto. Whapuuuuuu... Ha...

In this new sense of freedom, every-thing is still rushing around, but no-thing is sticking to me. Some-thing of a wonder Aigh would never have thought possible.

Whapuuuuuu... Ha... Whapuuuuuu... Ha... Whapuuuuuu... Ha...

Aigh see every-thing with the Blind I's of faith's courage, with a knoing sense that the peaceful wonder of accepting "not knoing," in lieu of the restrictive resistance of fearing what "I don't kno," is something Aigh've always known, and thought nothing of.

Imagine that...

Ha... Whapuuuuuu...

Peace and Courage to all beings of the realm

Aigh...

Journaling Page

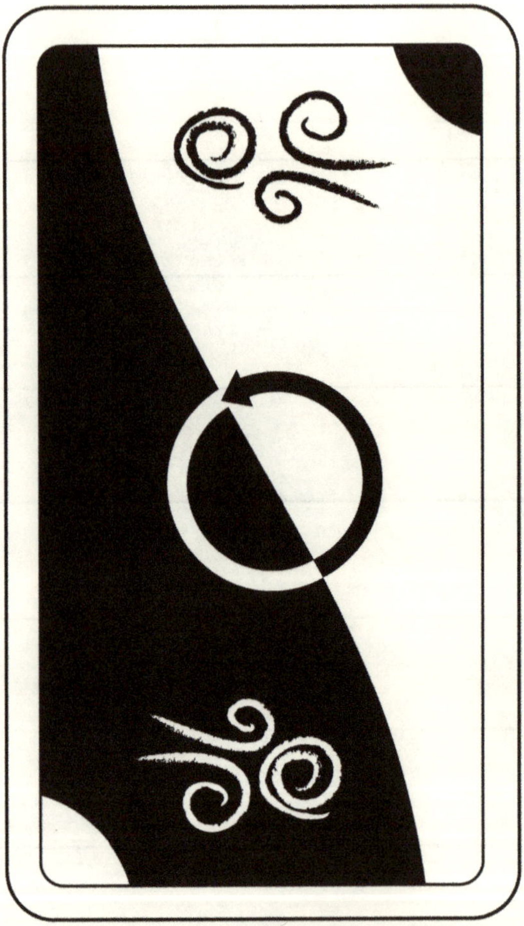

T.S. Eliot's Truth

Sub-deck: Notions

T.S. Eliot's Truth

Whapuuuuuu… Ha…

"We must never cease from exploration. And… the end of all our exploring will be to arrive where we began, only to know the place for the first time."

Whapuuuuuu… Ha… Whapuuuuuu… Ha…

It's a small wonder Aigh sense déjà vu every once in a while; no-wonder's the reason Aigh can't see to step into what Aigh already kno.

Imagine that…

Whapuuuuuu… Ha… Whapuuuuuu… Ha…
Whapuuuuuu… Ha…

So… in YinYang, wondering beyond what I think "I kno" is right, Aigh'm at home, knoing, Aigh've been down this road before, breathing peacefully in the knowledge - Aigh'm not alone in this.

Imagine that...

Ha… Whapuuuuuu…

Peace and Courage to all beings of the realm

Aigh…

It's a Black & White "thing"
No-wonder!

Sub-deck: Story

It's a Black & White "thing" No-wonder!

BLACK

WHITE

In the beginning it all seemed so simple, Black & White, no-wonder. So much so, I think nothing of labeling two sides. No big deal, "it's" two separate "things," anyone can see that.

BLACK

WHITE

Next comes drawing the box of what I think "I kno" is right about everything. Now "I don't kno" about you, but something about that thought makes me wonder. Intuitively, I shade what "I don't kno" dark, so the light of what I think "I kno" is right is all I'm open to see.

Suddenly one day, nothing seems like “it” any more. Naturally, chaos ensues, spiraling me counter to what I thought was right. No-wonder the Black & White mirror images blur as I spin by, seeing something about everything differently. And... Aigh realize “it” just may be no-thing I have ever thought to imagine before.

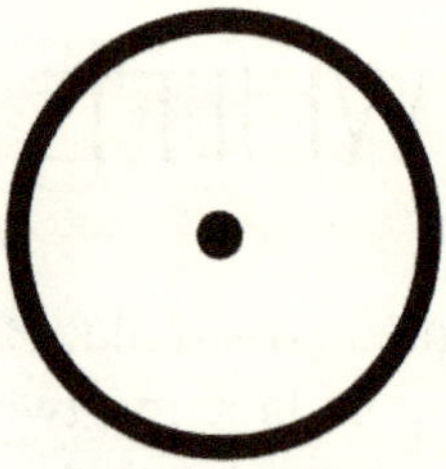

Having gone round-n-round with “things,” I’ve come to a point where Aigh feel open at my center. Feeling like Aigh can catch my breath at last, some-thing is happening to me, because no-thing seems to look like before, and every-thing is making another kind of sense, as this whole “thing” takes on a different kind of a familiar shape.

Blessed to be split by the G_od sense of a wavy sign of faith, Aigh feel the peace of G_od faith’s courage to open to some-thing of AnotherOne’s perspective. Drawing on my own G_od sense of “things,” Aigh follow the path before me.

In light of what I think, I shadow what I fear "I don't kno." Not knoing what to fear, Aigh wonder where this is heading. "It's" a small wonder Aigh'm not scared to death about the "things" Aigh'm hearing in the moment.

"It's" the courage to hold onto One's faith religiously enough, in order to let go of "things," opening both eyes to a common sign of G_od faith Aigh have known since Aigh can remember. Balanced by a G_od sense Aigh can hold onto, that's common enough as any one "thing" to remember, Aigh see insightfully beyond the labels Aigh started with.

"It's" a small wonder this stuff seems to go round-n-round. "It" isn't till Aigh opened my eyes, to see an outlook that resonates balance, in a way Aigh simply kno, for some odd reason. Not knoing is why, but that sounds crazy, as it should in YinYang, to what I thought I knew was right about "things" I thought were, simply, Black & White. It's wonder-full to finally see "it," this "thing" called G_od faith. Is seeing - believing? It's not knoing... that's the truth as Aigh've come to kno "it."

Imagine that...

Peace and Courage to all beings of the realm

Aigh...

Ok, five words or less

Sub-deck: Story

Ok, five words or less

Whapuuuuuu… Ha…

Another: Whapuuuuuu… I don't want to sound dense or any-"thing," but can some-One sum up all these "things" in five words or less? "I kno" I don't have time for all this nonsense, so, just bottom-line it for me. I think "I kno" where you're going, anyway. "I kno" I've listened to some-"thing" this WooWoo… before.

One: Ha… sure, but Aigh must warn Another that the answer should and will most likely sound "crazy," like non-sense, if it really is "not knoing," at first. The fact that you're looking further, wondering beyond what is known, to hear this, is wonder-full, in and of itself. Aigh would call it an act of G_od faith, but then again, that's just my G_od sense of "things."

If Aigh should get too far out, too quickly, and you find yourself lost, seeking the answers in the "right" order, look into the YinYang of two "things" for insight.

Whapuuuuuu… Ha… Whapuuuuuu… Ha…

Two "things" to remember as we start:

a) What sounds like non-sense in YinYang resonates with common sense.

b) To see what you want, One must start at the bottom and look up.

Aigh…

Peace and Courage to all beings of the realm

Ha… Whapuuuuuu…

Imagine that…

Small wonders may never cease again…

See… you've always known how to do this, we're back to where we started - naturally.

Whapuuuuuu… Ha… Whapuuuuuu… Ha…
Whapuuuuuu… Ha…

Isn't it some-thing that every-thing that resonates like non-sense makes common sense in the YinYang of "things?" It's literally "no-wonder" that keeps Another in fear of what "I don't kno" beyond what I think "I kno" is right… The answers are some-thing of a destination on a journey that's like no-thing Aigh could've thought to imagine… every-thing being like - truth!

1) Aigh…
2) Aigh'm speechless (Whapuuuuuu... Ha...)
3) Peace, Love, Joy
4) Aigh wonder… and you?
5) One's heart knos the truth

Ok, five words or less – here goes.

This makes nothing but non-sense when read out of order - it's no-wonder – really!

Journaling Page

What was, what may be & what is

Sub-deck: Story

What was, what may be & what is

Whapuuuuuu... Ha...

"what was" has passed to recall. It's having the courage of faith to see the insights in reflection of what I thought I knew was right at the time.

Whapuuuuuu... Ha... Whapuuuuuu... Ha...

"what may be" - is not knoing. And... the thing that matters here is the G_od sense Aigh get from trusting G_od faith to see me through to what's next. I fear what "I don't kno." Not knoing what to fear, Aigh'm ready for any-thing in the scheme of "things."

Whapuuuuuu... Ha... Whapuuuuuu... Ha...
Whapuuuuuu... Ha...

"what is" - is the reflection of my insightful outlook as it touches the world. Knoing there will be "things" to surrender as Aigh go, it's the strength of G_od faith that mirrors the G_od sense Aigh feel drawn to. Intuitively knoing one "thing" in the scheme of "things," some-thing about every-thing I think "I kno" is right, is like no-thing One can think to imagine in YinYang. It's no-wonder this stuff sounds crazy in the first moments, but resonates in a settling way, Aigh just kno, for some odd reason.

And... in reflection of all these "things," Aigh see "it" really is - not knoing...

Imagine that...

Ha... Whapuuuuuu...

Peace and Courage to all beings of the realm

Aigh…

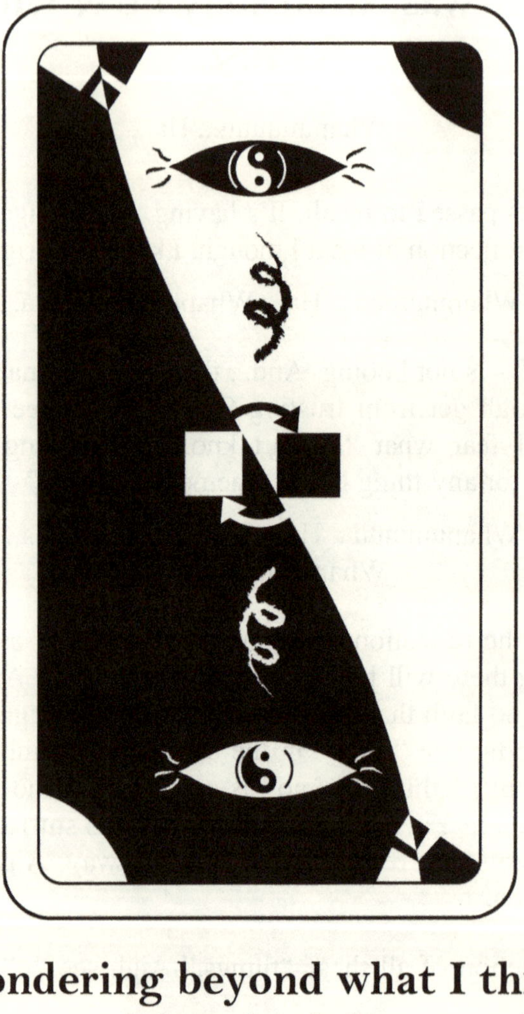

**Wondering beyond what I think
I kno is right**

Sub-deck: Story

Wondering beyond what I think I kno is right

Whapuuuuuu... Ha...

Now, One may be thinking, who in their "right" mind is going to venture there, knoing their thoughts are going to be published? I can't think to imagine who, but it's no-wonder that Aigh'm thought to be crazy "enough." So, here goes...

In truth, I'm afraid "I don't kno" what Aigh must be thinking, to risk everything, to come out, not knoing if the notion of reflecting beyond what I think "I kno" is right, is worth any-"thing" in the scheme of "things," or just more non-sense.

Wondering on, Aigh see what's thought to be safe, in the reflection of the Ones standing in mass, in fear of daring to step out. It's no-wonder, the mere thought of opening to some-thing beyond every-thing I think "I kno" is "right," is no-thing short of scary – truth!

The small wonder One gets from wandering outside the box of "I kno," is the peace of free breath, knoing some-"things" are meant to be not knoing, opening One to no-thing short of G_od faith, as every-thing appears different, in light of what I thought I knew to be right. A true G_od sense.

And... in the YinYang of migh reflection, what sounded like non-sense resonates with common sense, so if One wonders beyond what they think, their insight alters their outlook. In view of every-thing, from this perspective, some-thing seems to balance "things" like no-"thing" "I kno" I've thought of before. Imagine that...

"I don't kno" what I was so afraid of; wondering beyond what "I kno" is no-thing more than opening to some-thing, in light of every-thing I think is right, in G_od faith another perspective will aid in balancing migh insight, in the scheme of "things," not knoing what's next in the reflection of a wondered outlook.

May this reflection of peace, love and joy be ever with you.

Ha… Whapuuuuuu…

Peace and Courage to all beings of the realm

Aigh…

Journaling Page

Common Thread

Sub-deck: a Book that is

Common Thread

No two things can be entirely dissimilar by the fact that they have a dissimilarity to unite them in sameness.

And no two things can be entirely the same by the very fact that they would be one thing by the entire unity of the same.

This unity of being is the cohesive bond of the One.

May I forever take peace in Its liberating dominion.

Man's World

Sub-deck: a Book that is

Man's World

It is now accepted by many that man's[1] nature and psychology interpret and present raw sensory data into understandable ideas, creating a subjective experience of reality. While this experience is subjective, it is the product of an essential humanity and an independent reality that affects the subjective experience. Here I wish to discuss the first of these non-accidental realities: the Human Spirit. Old psychologists have proposed an essential sex drive, and modern cynics call it greed, but these are just accidental expressions of this human nature (which is all too varied, as psychologists have found out). Now wouldn't it be just peachy if I could give some clear phrase that you could read off this page and come to know yourself, but it is a sheer farce that I could have such power.

Such an answer is found on the horizons of yourself and your world, which for these purposes are one and the same, yourself being experienced through your world. So strive for what would content your soul, and not what was for your fathers, and is in society, and in the end, you shall find your true self.

Why leave the whims of your deepest beliefs, of your heart and soul, to those around you? Are they so well instructed?

However, here know this, that a man is nothing without his fathers and brothers. So always respect and consider those you depend on, and those that depend on you. May I also say, to blind one's eye to a grief of one's heart is not the same as tending it.

My faith here requires of me that I implore you to remembrance of the One as the father of fathers, for through such may you find yourself on the straight path, where all signs may come to be known.

May I forever take peace in Its liberating dominion.

---

[1] I here and elsewhere use 'man' as short for human, and in no way do I wish to imply that what I discuss only applies to males of our species. Other male classifiers used are also intended to be gender neutral and express all humans of a certain relation.

What makes a man?

Sub-deck: a Book that is

What makes a man?

What makes a man? Or for that matter a bird, or a fish, or a tree? Some would like to say it's chemical properties and physical makeup, but I feel that something may go unappreciated with such an explanation. The mind is what I fear lacks acknowledgement in that simple answer. This is obvious when one considers how a living being is formed. It is not the physical structure that comes first, but rather the instructions for building such a structure. Here the skeptics will smirk, and jeer such a fool that does not see that these instructions are in the form of chemical strands called DNA. However, I would again implore you ask - how is DNA formed?

Statistics have shown us that this process cannot possibly be random. This means that some purpose has driven all of the generations of our species, as well as any other. And what is biological ability but the emergent behavior of cooperative processes. The abilities and motivations generated by this purpose I call the mind. For what is an arm without that which moves it? The traditional purpose given is survival. This I feel is an antiquated outlook when you are discussing humans. For as a species, our survival is not threatened by anything other than ourselves.

Here we are, with all that was instilled into the human mind over generations of "animal" survival. Shall we not then seek new purpose for such remnants, abilities already possessed by us? Why think evolution makes man as a beast? I feel blessed that our intellect was what brought about out dominance and stability, for it is such a fun toy now![2]

Returning to my original question, what makes a human or any living thing? I have stressed a kind of mind, but let us not reject the physical, nor the union of the two that is our experience. Why blind one's eye to signs readily apparent? Why divide the two, because someone has the audacity to deny that which cannot be seen, but is

[2] But it still has work to do, and this is all too obvious.

self-evident? Why forget your history and despise your vehicle? Let us leave this nonsense and appreciate what **is**. For all is Good, nothing without corrupts the man, only that which comes from within corrupts. Then may we see the beauty that is in the beast, and in the brush, and in ourselves.

May I forever take peace in Its liberating dominion.

Journaling Page

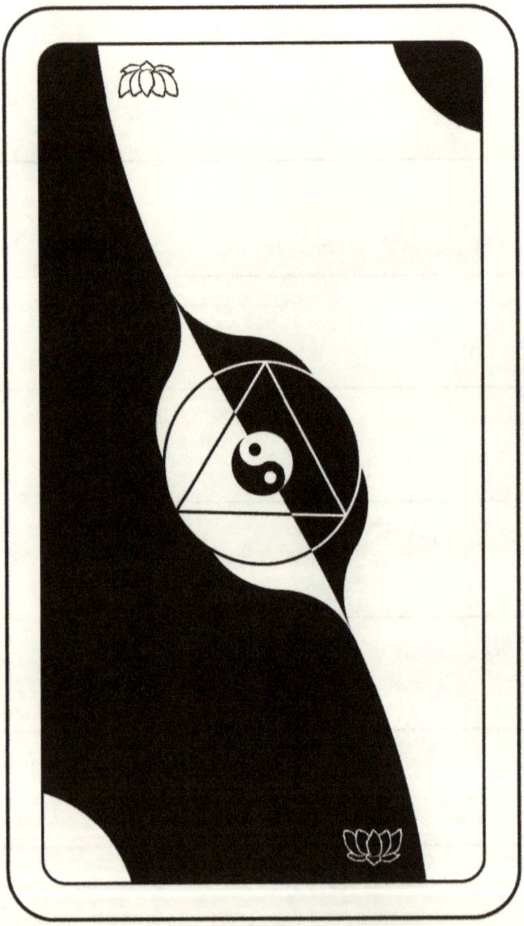

Third-Eye's Insight

Sub-deck: Chakras

Third-Eye (Ajna) Chakra

Location:	at the level center of the forehead
Meaning:	conscious awareness, center of wonder
Pronounced:	Aj-na
Color:	deep indigo
Petals:	two
Element:	insight of outlook
Receptor:	Aigh
Sense:	extra sensory perception
Endocrine gland:	pituitary gland

Flowing signs possess the Third-Eye's insight of outlook. Seeing what's hidden in plane sight of the moon's cycle, the Aigh gets a knoing sense from its extrasensory reading of the pattern of evolution, manifesting the "pop" of Infinity's Loop, as it sees the dots line up in YinYang. In the realm of spirit, the Aigh sees free breath in the dawning light of its sponsoring notion.

Naturally and intuitively flowing signs: Sagittarius, Scorpio and Pisces.

Resistant signs firmly stand in the perception of outlook's physical image. Deaf from the drone of chaos's swirling cycle of inner static, restricted in breath and frozen in the moon's cycle, the Aigh sees claims of some-thing touching every-thing, as no-thing but a story told in the dark with a light on. Blind to what's hiding in plane sight it stands, swirled in its own flow.

Naturally and intuitively resistant signs: Aries, Taurus, Leo, Virgo and Capricorn.

Neutral signs sense the swirl of restricted breath, as the Aigh blinks open in a moment of peace. Gasping for a breath, the Aigh fears voicing its recall of sight, thinking the wonder of its vision sounds crazy. In terror of "not knoing," the Aigh clings to resistance, beating its-self to surrender.

Naturally and intuitively neutral signs: Gemini, Cancer, Libra and Aquarius.

Seeking a clear healing in the crystal's vibrating chants, in the silence of no-thing, just may stir some-thing, altering every-thing that choice is yours.

Peace and Courage to all beings of the realm

Aigh…

Journaling Page

A recollection of space and time

Sub-deck: Cosmic Herald

A recollection of space and time

Floating dreams of Philosophers and fools,
Is the life you seek beyond your tools?
In sight of home we live with science,
But is it truth, or man's appliance?
Can you know the things which can't be thought?
Can you know for sure that you can not?
In slumber we rule the dimensions three,
But if one wakes, what comes to be?
Can you see the thunder of speculation,
The veil of reason and calculation?
What would it be if you could know?
Break free of thought and join the flow.
The beauty of cosmos, it shall be known,
For it is born of soul and soul alone.
Then you will see the truth, and you will find,
That truth is nothing more that existence defined.
And with great joy, my final rhyme,
A recollection of space and time.

Peace

Dawn of what's next

Sub-deck: Cosmic Herald

Dawn of what's next

Soft dancing gypsy eyes they wander through the summer night
Where slumbering premonitions of the dead awake
And where lust is born of the streets and allies, creeping into your window with delusions of omnipotent rage.
For death lies not at the end of a blade, but in the word your lover speaks.
Sleep, once more, let fanciful visions occupy your sight
And so the day retreats to night.

Simple people who need not know my secrets
They populate the villages and hamlets of days long past.
The armored rider and his kinetic serenade
Burst into existence from paths so far untraveled
The fabric of time can be unraveled.

Forgotten gods and ancient thrones have not a care for earthly hymns.
Yes they do indeed travel to the realms of fantasy
To the dominion of the Sun King where lives the heart of all mankind
And to the lands which lie between this world, and those not quite adjacent.
Such is the plight of man, who against his will awakes,
For soft light through an eastern window breaks
And so he does pay for all that he takes.

Peace

Fire

Sub-deck: Cosmic Herald

Fire

The flame is wanting.
It is he who burns but is not consumed.
Apart from wick,
Apart from air
His birth is death
And his death, birth.
The flame is wanting,
Taking in all he sees,
But in doing so he shall learn truly
What wanting is,
For when all to be had is had,
He must find that in consuming all
He has left his universe empty
And no longer can even he exist

But in his dying moment he must remember
The air and the wick
Who give of themselves freely,
For they realize that they are born of the space between atoms,
The space between electrons and nucleus.
Yes it is they who realize that they are born of empty space,
That they are nothing
And… that they want for nothing
And that matter is only the fuel for wanting.
Yes it is only he who realizes that he occupies empty space who can
truly make full himself.

Peace

For fear of darkness or fear of light?

Sub-deck: Cosmic Herald

For fear of darkness or fear of light?

Sweet darkness of the newest moon
Newer still with each moment of being
And newer still as the ladies swoon
For fear of darkness or fear of light?

Embrace the heavens for they are cause
Of all the light so fondly forgotten
But this newest moon must give us pause
The cosmos do not yearn my thanks

And so long forgotten the words of men
Who weep to hear the mourning bell
To think of what they could have been
And softer still returns the night

For across the shores of the river Seine
I drifted off to win my rest
To think of all my fleshed pain
As I lay upon these darkened banks
For fear of darkness or fear of light?

The cosmos do not yearn my thanks
And softer still returns the night
As I lay upon these darkened banks

So sheltered from the realm of sight
For fear of darkness or fear of light?

Peace

Silent Judge

Sub-deck: Cosmic Herald

Silent Judge

I spoke for sixteen nights and days
Without uttering a word.
When so stately perched upon my nose,
A vagrant, whistlin' bird,
Crying "Alack, Alack! My boisterous sir,
Please tell me have you heard
Of the man who spoke for sixteen days,
Without uttering a word."

"I do believe that I am he,"
I said in sportish humor.
"Although it's hard to distinguish fact,
from fiction or from rumor.
For my lovely wife, so new departed,
They surely did exhume her
And they claimed that with a jealous hand
And heart did I so doom her."

He did not answer me, this bird,
But gave a piercing glare.
The evidence, I hid so well,
It surely wasn't there.
No prints I left upon her, no,
I lifted them with care.
But in his gaze I could see myself
Going down that icy stair.

"Do not be so quick to pass
Your judgment on my broken soul,
For it was she who was not true to me.
She abused my trust; she lied and stole
My youth, which I did deed to her,

When another man she did love in whole.
But before I killed her, I'll have you know,
Two coins I gave for the Boatman's toll.

For sixteen nights and days I spoke
Before twelve men so true and fair
And though deaf they were, I could not escape
The whistling bird on a kitchen chair.
For my deeds did prove too much to bear
In the face of his blank and somber glare.
So for sixteen nights and days I sank, to the bottom of the sea
And all the pretty fishes were staring back at me.

Peace

Journaling Page

The Dreamer

Sub-Deck: Cosmic Herald

The Dreamer

Dream by day and dream by night
All our fears are out of sight.
Waiting in the shadow for
A chance to creep into the door,
Of the soul and of the mind,
Of all the secrets, revealed in time.
The beasts are desperate to devour
The tears of those who shy and cower.

Dream by night and dream by day.
The woeful spirits, they long to say,
"Heed my call and don't pass me by
Or else this day is the day you die!"
And though the warning, it goes unspoken,
The soul can listen, through bonds unbroken,
By heaven and hell and the mourning bell,
It seems to cry…
"Today's the Day!"
"Today we fly!"

Dream in living and dream in dying,
The golden herald is a-crying
To those with minds that are not closed
To fearsome thoughts which are proposed
By a mind of freedom, a mind of joy.
The fears instilled are just a toy
To the puppeteer and puppet too,
Who long to turn a shade of blue,
To live in peace with earth and sky,
A peace unseen by the naked eye.

Dream in dying and dream in living.
The heart so pure is all forgiving,
The heart of ice will quell the flame,
And who shall live, to take the blame?
With smoke and mirrors and thoughts unknown,
The truth in being is always shown.

Dream of love and dream of sorrow.
Hold so gently the time you borrow.
For those who live without a dream,
Live a lie, or so it seems.
But those who dream in misty wonder
Can brave the storm of rain and thunder.

Peace

Journaling Page

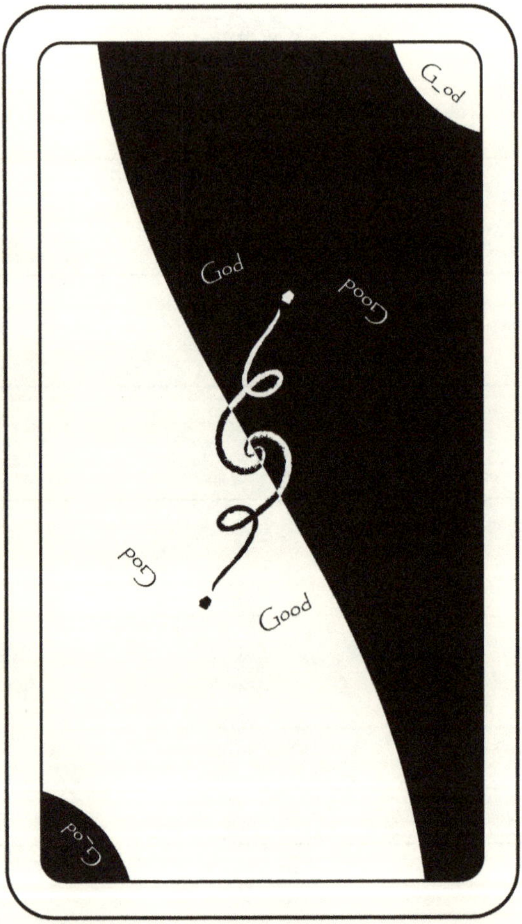

Good or God?

Sub-deck: G_od sense

Good or God?

Whapuuuuuu… Ha…

Another: Is G_od… good or god?

One: It's not knoing…

Another: Not knoing?

One: Exactly.

Another: "I kno" what exactly means, what "I don't kno" is what you mean by exactly. And… if I heard you correctly, you "more or less" evaded what I see as an answer. So… tell me straight up - is it good or god?

One: Both.

Another: Now wait a minute, exactly what do you mean by that?!

One: Aigh have faith that a hand of good intention is what any god's sense of light in aid of another "is." So to aid in freeing the breath of another, in G_od faith, Aigh'm offering to share migh sense of One god in good faith – awakening to a G_od sense of another. From this plane, Aigh go forward with good faith, and when Aigh'm in less than god sense, Aigh have the peace of knoing Aigh'm going in the "right" direction.

Whapuuuuuu… Ha… Whapuuuuuu… Ha…

Another: So… it's religious – right?

One: It's not knoing… but if the shining light of your religious faith is extended trustfully in your god's highest sense, paving way because you're "right," you are "more or less" short of seeing a G_od faith connection. Yes… there are those who have to "be" religiously right, blind to the hidden connections of what they agree on. In the end, it all depends on your perception of my insight's outlook, and that is truly not knoing to me. What's true is within One's own reflection.

Another: So… what if I have common faith without religion, what is G_od then?

One: It's not knoing… If the insight of your outlook is clearly resonating what's true in your heart, extending your hand in good faith to another, attempting to build a bridge, manifesting a rock solid connection, my sense is One is seeing the light, and that may be both a good and god sense, as the lines converge into a sense of One.

Another: So… why the confusing G_od spelling?

One: It's not knoing… whether or not G_od is good or god at any moment, the lines are likely to blur as One flows between. As One follows their path, extending a hand of good intention to all, the sense of being in the light of god's grace resonates in return, with a knoing sense of an honest connection of trust. For example: while One may think it's more prudent to safeguard a half empty glass in fear of having "not enough," in the wonder of viewing the same glass as half full, One is less likely to fear sharing the abundance, giving in good faith, with a knoing awareness of god's resonation filling the glass in a G_od way.

Whapuuuuuu… Ha… Whapuuuuuu… Ha…

Whapuuuuuu… Ha…

Another: Is there a bottom line to this? Migh head feels light and G_od right now.

One: Truth – it's not knoing… but to speak it plainly, Aigh'd say- if One offers good intentions faithfully to all and is filled by a good sense resonating in return, manifesting a good feeling inside, then that's a good thing. Exchanging the word god for good takes One to a similar place, so you see, it really is… not knoing.

Another: Then I guess it's a G_od thing I asked - right?

One: Yes… Imagine that…

Ha… Whapuuuuuu…

Peace and Courage to all beings of the realm

Aigh…

I kno

Sub-deck: Knoings

I kno

I stopped to wonder one day: What do I really kno?

By that, I mean in a way that it can't be refuted by science, religion, urban myth, folklore, ancient scrolls, wall carvings, etc., all the way to the first inclination of an organized notion that life might be—nothing.

Wow, I love a good mind—bender.

Hmm… Well… "I kno" I'm here.

But if queried: Where's here? I can only say now.

Hmm… Where's now? Oops, It's gone!

Hmm… So, my sense of "Aigh" is all that seems to be left, and if you think about it, isn't that some-thing that looks like no-thing that is the essence of every-thing?

Yeah… "I kno" no-thing, it's been with me since not knoing...

Ha… Whapuuuuuu…

Peace and Courage to all beings of the realm

Aigh…

I don't kno

Sub-deck: Knoings

I don't kno

I stopped to wonder the one day and I found out "I kno" nothing. How on earth could I stop there?

Hmm… So, now I'm a skeptic whose question is: "What don't I kno?"

Hmm… "I don't kno… I don't kno…. I don't kno what I DON'T KNO!"

Whapuuuuuu… Ha…

So… where am I now? I'm gonna need a few breaths to get myself clear on where I am – because "I don't kno."

Whapuuuuuu… Ha… Whapuuuuuu… Ha…
Whapuuuuuu… Ha…

Hmm… Let's see if I'm clear so far. I really don't kno, what "I don't kno." But I do kno some-thing about no-thing being the essence of every-thing. And that it has been with me since "not knoing."

Whapuuuuuu… Wow… Aigh really am on the other side of the looking glass now.

So… Aigh'm here, wondering what Aigh should have faith in, since "I don't kno."

Hmm… Whapuuuuuu… My sense is to surrender to the "not knoing," that can't be refuted, that's been with me since origin, and is the path that's always been in front of me through the ages.

Hmm… Wow…

Peace and Courage to all beings of the realm

Aigh…

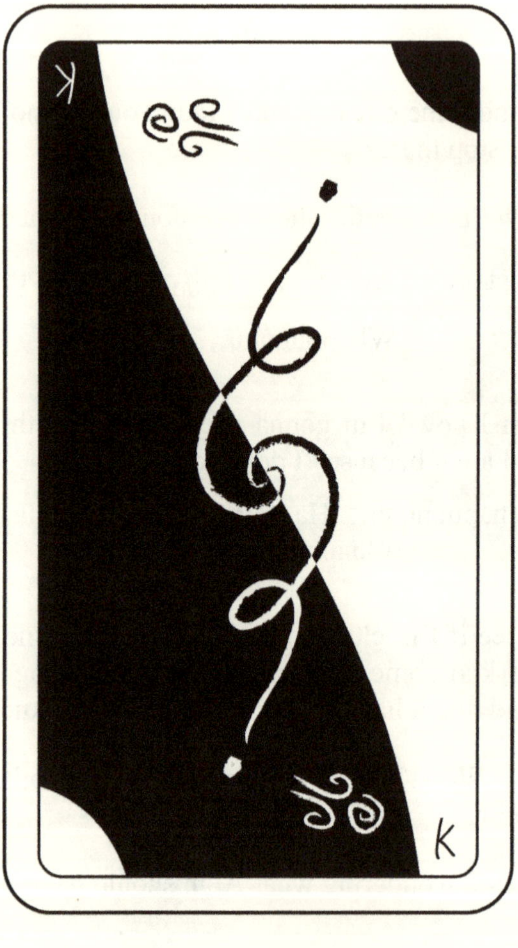

Not knoing…

Sub-deck: Knoings

Not knoing…

Another:	Aigh stopped to wonder the one day, and Aigh found out "I kno" no-thing. Aigh stopped to wonder the next day and found out "I don't kno what I don't kno" about no-thing.
AnotherOne:	Whapuuuuuu… Ha…
Another:	So, where am Aigh now?
One:	Whapuuuuuu … It's not knoing…. Ha…
Another:	Now Aigh'm surrendering to "not knoing…" Whapuuuuuu … Ha… Hmm… So… What's Next?
One:	Whapuuuuuu… It's not knoing…. Ha…
Another:	Hmm… So… Where's now?
One:	Whapuuuuuu… It's not knoing…. Ha…
Another:	Hmm… Yeah… Aigh found now - Aigh'm experiencing unreasonable joy at the moment, from the free breath of being conscious to the notion, that the essence of every-thing, that was the start of some-thing, from no-thing, and has been around since "not knoing"— is me.

From here, Aigh sense my faith extends in the infinite loop that springs from the origin — me again. Aigh am the essence of every-thing spawned from no-thing, into some-thing Aigh manifest.

Imagine that…

From here Aigh sense a place of Knoing.

Ha… Whapuuuuuu … Hmm…

Peace and Courage to all beings of the realm

Aigh…

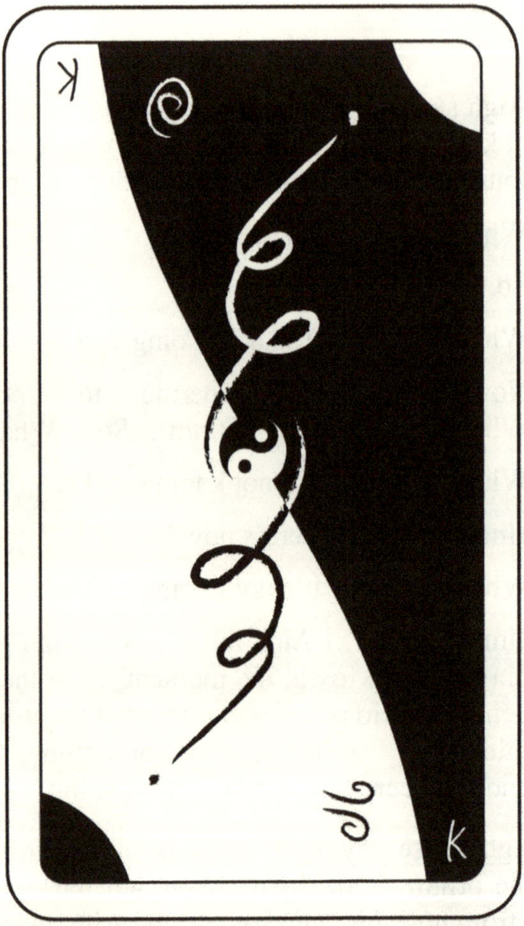

Knoing

Sub-deck: Knoings

Knoing

Wow, three days past Aigh consciously began a journey through the ages.

First, "I kno" nothing. Then, "I don't kno what I don't kno" about nothing. So Aigh surrendered to "not knoing…" no-thing to learn the knoing of peace, love and joy of the juuju of the essence of every-thing—is me.

Whapuuuuuu … Yeah… Whapuuuuuu … Aigh…
Whapuuuuuu… Ha...

Hmm … Aigh'm humbled to kno Aigh come from as far back as nothing, and yet Aigh'm here now to share this notion of some-thing from the essence of the origin of every-thing. Knoing Aigh am One in the same, Aigh sense my faith has reached across the realm, infinitely connected to the origin of nothing, and Aigh am at peace, for "Aigh kno" the depth of my being.

Yeah… "Aigh kno" no-thing, it's where Aigh started - not knoing…

Knoings emerge from not knoing…

Ha… Whapuuuuuu…

Peace and Courage to all beings of the realm

Aigh…

Knock… Knock…

Sub-deck: Musings

Knock… Knock…

Another:	Who's there...?
One:	Oh... it's just me...
Another:	Oh... it's just me... who?
One:	You knos who, Aigh
Another:	You knos who, Aigh - who?
One:	Aigh who knos you, that's who!
Another:	OMG... it's no-wonder! Why didn't you say so in the first place?
One:	Aigh did. It's just that Aigh sounded odd to you at first, so now you think Aigh'm crazy. So, naturally, it just follows that you'd have to wonder if Aigh'm nuts, which is true from one perspective, but not from many others.
Another:	Really... Ok... so which is it then - crazy or nuts?
One:	Oh... it's not knoing... But my sense is Aigh'd be nuts to think no-wonder is just too crazy to grasp. What would be at risk, daring to wander open minded, wondering insightfully, listening in order to hear the truth of some-thing from within?
Another:	Oh... I must be nuts to even be thinking of some-thing that sounds this crazy!
One:	G_od... Aigh thought we'd never get here!

Another: Here!? And... where exactly are we?!

One: Ahhh... Aigh forgot - it's no-wonder. Ok - so hear what Aigh think. Aigh'm nuts for speaking what you'd be crazy to even consider listening to. And... Aigh'd have to be crazy to think sounding this way would do anything less than make you nuts after hearing it. So you see, we're both nuts at this point, and the crazy thing about it is - it makes sense.

Another: Boy... what was I thinking before opening this door?

One: Oh... Aigh was wondering that myself. It's funny how some-thing as simple as a knock can open a door that leads to a common point even if "it" sounds crazy at first thought. One would have to be nuts not to hear the sound of it calling as it resonates through one of life's closed doors.

Another: Right... I think I hear the phone ringing...

One: Aigh wonder who that could be? Ya kno, it's no-wonder you're hearing things again, and you think Aigh'm nuts. Imagine that...

Peace and Courage to all beings of the realm

Aigh...

Journaling Page

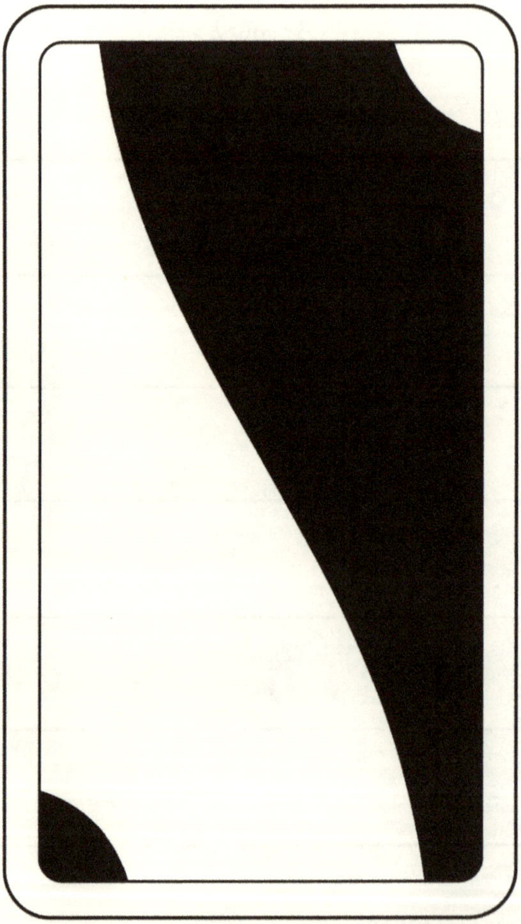

Clean Slate

Sub-deck: Notions

Clean Slate

So... there has to be a point to something, or everything that follows means nothing, the way Ego's I thinks. And... if not knoing… everything means some-thing balances like no - "thing" Aigh've come to before, while breathing peacefully, then wouldn't it behoove me to look a little further? Aigh wonder... and you?

Clean Slate is the "Do Over" card of the realm. Ever in the mix, it comes to all at the "right" time. Knoing when is not important; being ready to read "it" when "it" comes - is. And... as crazy as that may sound, the G_od sense of turning to G_od faith is that "it" resonates beyond religious ties, to light what's next.

Whapuuuuuu... Ha... Whapuuuuuu... Ha...

One can choose to alter one "thing" or another, in a turn of T.S. Eliot's truth. If Aigh were to choose some-thing over another, with no-thing to lose but the fear of what "I don't kno," trusting not knoing… would sound like a G_od "thing." Seeing insightout, every-thing beyond, in G_od faith, really is some-thing different, because no-thing seems impossible in YinYang.

Coming to kno this peace is like no-thing that can be purchased, unlike every-thing "I kno" I've been struggling to hang onto. What would be at risk to be free of some-thing like that? Free from burden's weight, One can see how some-thing like a practiced breath is like no-thing I thought I had time for, while every-thing seems at peace, in the midst of chaos surrounding me at times.

One can choose to wander through the mirror, wondering at the mix of reflections, living to die, or One could think to imagine dying to live as the only way to see the light. In the end, the difference is: One will take “its” last breath in peace, and the other will drop from the fear of holding on to “its” last gasp.

Whapuuuuuu... Ha... Whapuuuuuu... Ha... Whapuuuuuu... Ha...

And... if One could take three slow deep breaths in G_od faith, to step in, secure, knoing “it” only takes one slow deep breath in YinYang to find the G_od sense of stepping out, peacefully, from a wonder Aigh’ll live to remember - would it be worth the risk?

My sense: Yes… My truth: it’s not knoing... My being: Whapuuuuuu... Ha...

All spirits really do choose...

It’s what would be next... the challenge of the journey is One of a kind.

Imagine that... in G_od faith, and a G_od sense will follow.

Ha... Whapuuuuuu...

Peace and Courage to all beings of the realm

Aigh...

Journaling Page

Insightout

Sub-deck: Notions

Insightout

Whapuuuuuu… Ha…

Aigh recently spent some time with AnotherOne, pondering no wonder. Aigh found the stickiness between was the fear of my reflection in AnotherOne's eyes and the oddity in the order of my speech. Knoing mere words between us could not say enough, Aigh sent pictures along, reflecting a range of my likenesses.

Ever mirroring the other, we see OneAnother from across the extremes. It's no-wonder that blinds One from Another's insight into an opposing view. Resisting every-thing out of habit, some-thing beyond what I think "I kno," is no-thing but a dayDream in the scheme of "things."

Whapuuuuuu… Ha… Whapuuuuuu… Ha…

Starting with a colored image, Aigh captured a likeness of myself lost in a dayDream. As we wondered along with OneAnother, down the path of no-wonder, Aigh shot an image in negative with my eyes blinded by the shadow of what I think "I kno." What "I don't kno" is why the light of my soul shines through the darkness in G_od faith, even though my eyes are veiled.

Flashing to the other extreme, Aigh appeared all aglow in the warmth of juuju's loving waves, resonating from my soul. Blushing a scarlet hue, the divine envelops me as Aigh long to express the essence of who Aigh am.

Seeking the balance between, my image pinches in the middle, generating a crazy effect as Aigh laugh at the notion of how nuts being balanced can seem to Another from the other side of the looking glass at first.

In a vain effort to gain notice, Aigh next sent some brochure shots to demonstrate proof of my adventures. Unmoved by the poses, Another asked for nothing more than a basic shot in "real" time.

Never One to catch Another off guard, Aigh gave fair warning to be careful what is asked for, with an all too knoing glance from one of my common looks. Capturing just how boring peace, love and joy can appear as Aigh mugged for a tight shot.

Split any number of ways in a new moon's presence, Aigh see the face of AnotherOne in my reflection. Lost on the dark side of the moon, it took seeing the pyramids of my youth to point the way. So… naturally, no sojourn is complete without a walk on the dark side. Gandering up, Aigh come to see the shades of my caricature, knoing Aigh can choose to be any One of them.

Whapuuuuuu… Ha… Whapuuuuuu… Ha…
Whapuuuuuu… Ha…

Wondering exactly what's going on, One urges Another to pull "it" together, bringing the sight of my focus to One, once again. With a former image insight, Aigh'm close to the end of my journey, having come face to face with a younger self.

Asked for five words or less to explain all these "things" we've just gone through together, Aigh'd have to say; "It's not knoing… Whapuuuuuu… Ha…" as Aigh see signs of T.S. Eliot's truth, as we've gone Insightout, ending at the beginning, knoing the silver lines Aigh've come to kno have saged my outlook, in a way only G_od faith can.

The G_od sense Aigh get from G_od faith is in the peace and courage of my breath, as Aigh come to see the other sides of my being, knoing Aigh am but an image of reflection.

Imagine that…

Ha… Whapuuuuuu…

Peace and Courage to all beings of the realm

Aigh…

Journaling Page

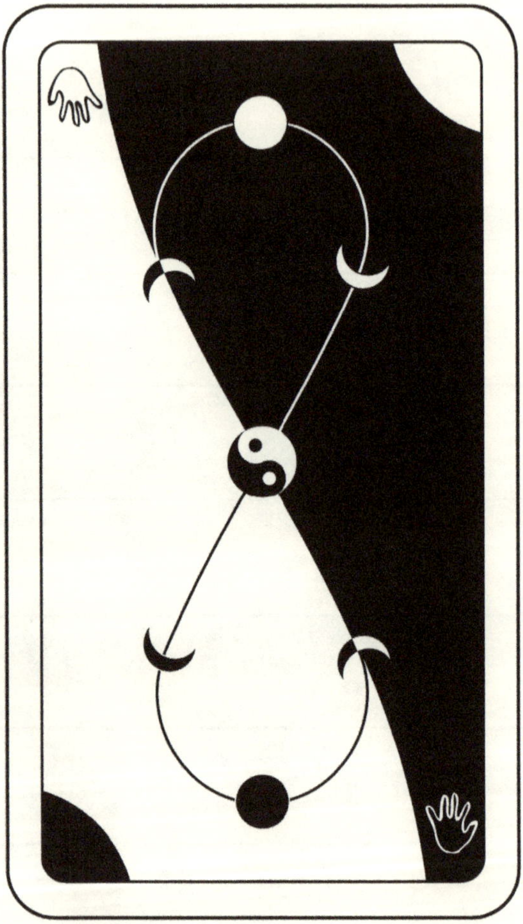

Sense of Balance

Sub-Deck: Senses

Sense of Balance

Whapuuuuuu… Ha…

something – nothing – everything

Lost in the chaos of Ego's I, some-thing about every-thing is no-thing "I kno" I can keep on fighting. Some-thing's gotta give, because every-thing has me wavering, and it seems no-thing I can think to imagine is settling "things."

Drawn to following the moon's cycle, Aigh come to see the extremes of its phases, naturally, since Aigh've been under it all of this life. It is here Aigh come to seek the balance between a new moon's hiding in plane site, to the height of my shadow being back lit by a full moon's presence.

Waxing my way counter to clockwise, Aigh see the first phase of YinYang, as if it has been staring me in the eye my whole life. Overwhelmed by its beauty, Aigh stop to catch my breath, feeling myself level off. Whapuuuuuu… Ha…

As the noise of Ego's I fades, Aigh can clearly see the extremes of what I think, and it's no-wonder Aigh fear the height of my shadow. Waning once again into YinYang, on the backside of the moon's cycle, Aigh come to the G_od sense of breathing, in light of the balanced image from above, not knoing what's next, as a new moon evolves in plane sight of what I hadn't thought to imagine before.

So… what's at risk in a sense of balance?

something – nothing – everything

Imagine that…

Whapuuuuuu… Ha… Whapuuuuuu… Ha…
Whapuuuuuu… Ha…

Peace and Courage to all beings of the realm

Aigh…

Journaling Page

Whapuuuuuu... Ha...

Sub-deck: Breaths

Whapuuuuuu… Ha…

Pronounced in any tongue: Wha pooo… Haaaaaa… is an ancient expression meaning peace of free breath. As a welcomed breath of greeting, it unites us in the cohesive bond of the One.

Said correctly, it sounds like your hearing's memory of the wind's voice, followed by the surrender to a breath of stillness - Whapuuuuuu… Ha… It's not knoing what it sounds like until you breathe into speaking it with intention. You'll see, when you hear it.

Whapuuuuuu... Ha... Whapuuuuuu... Ha...

Since every-thing must do some-thing, its purpose in no-thing is to gain your perspective. If you wondered what you think, wouldn't "what's next" be a different image in the mirror?

Migh sense: Yes… Migh truth: it's not knoing… Migh being: Whapuuuuuu… Ha…

What's at risk in the breath of "what's next?" It's not knoing, but migh sense from the origin is that migh essence has, is and will endure migh heart rock's journey. Aigh might as well share a free breath of peace as Aigh go.

Whapuuuuuu… Ha… Whapuuuuuu… Ha…
Whapuuuuuu… Ha…

Sound silly? Well… maybe… but think about it, when was the last time you gave some-thing of your sense of the light of every-thing, in a breath that was nothing of an effort?

Migh experience: it only takes One to get many breathing.

Imagine that…

Ha... Whapuuuuuu...

Peace and Courage to all beings of the realm

Aigh…

Non-Sense

Sub-deck: Story

Non-Sense

Whapuuuuuu... Ha...

Another: Talk about non-sense, this stuff makes no sense that "I kno" of. Sure... I get the slow deep breathing part, I just think it sounds weird, hearing it aloud. "I don't kno" what the big deal is, I'm afraid "things" like this are just a ruse that I have no faith in what-so-ever.

Whapuuuuuu... Ha... Whapuuuuuu... Ha...

One: It's not knoing that matters, and it's no-wonder this sounds like non-sense to you. It should, it would be what's next if you have no sense of this type of work. The slow deep breathing is to summon the courage of your faith, to wonder what you can't think to imagine. Hearing it resonate aloud, in the breath of your own G_od intention, is key, in the scheme of "things", when speaking of faith, don't you think?

Wondering any-thing, much less, faith, short of G_od intention, is worth nothing, as everything is shadowed by something that smells like cynicism. Caught, afraid of admitting what "I don't kno," the freedom of "not knoing" is nothing but a pipe dream. So... naturally, it only makes common sense that this sounds like non-sense to you.

And ... if this gives you some sense that we hear OneAnother, then a common sense is shared between us. In light of that, what's at risk to look further in the presence of your own G_od faith, to see if something else may be hiding in plane insight, of what One can't think to imagine?

Whapuuuuuu... Ha... Whapuuuuuu... Ha…
Whapuuuuuu... Ha...

There's no-thing "real" to lose when wondering beyond every-thing I think Ego's I knos. Besides, some-thing as simple as slow deep breathing really does settle "things" like no-thing else "Aigh kno," naturally does.

In light of this, One could say, intuitively, hearing non-sense, at first, has led to a G_od sense reflection of your own G_od faith. And... like that, some-thing came from no-thing to touch every-thing you hadn't thought to imagine, before.

Turning non-sense insightout makes common sense, when figuring all these "things" out. I never would've thought to imagine my own G_od faith would be the G_od sense Aigh'd get from this work, but it is.

Seeing no-thing as some-thing not to fear changes every-thing, in the scheme of "things," and as crazy as it may have sounded at first blush, an Image of Reflection is a G_od "thing" to wonder about - wouldn't you say?

Imagine that...

Ha... Whapuuuuuu...

Peace and Courage to all beings of the realm

Aigh...

Journaling Page

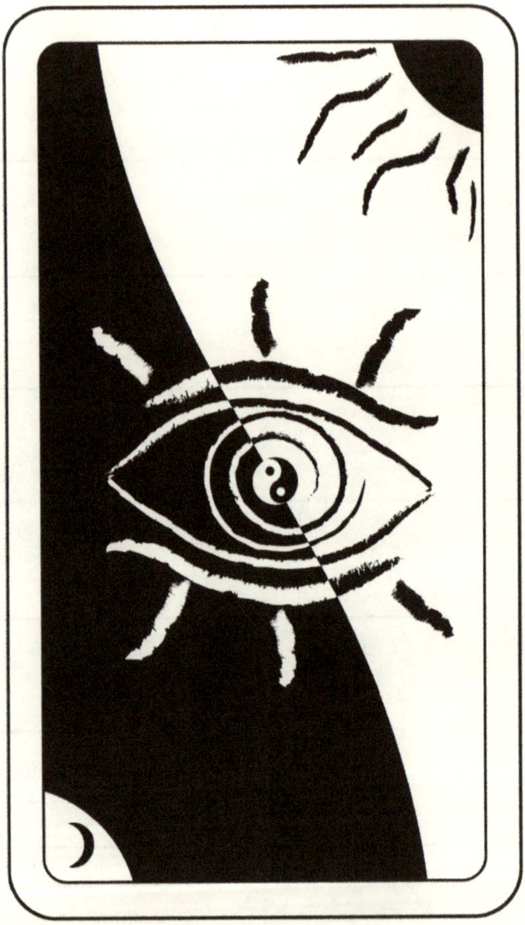

Wild Eye 1: Origin-al Eye

Sub-deck: Wild Eyes

Wild Eye 1

Origin-al Eye

Whapuuuuuu... Ha...

Every-thing comes from some-thing, and no-thing I can think of comes to mind easily, when pondering One's beginning. It's with a newborn's perspective that One is meant to see the insight of this reading, for in "it" is a message from the origin.

It's not knoing what the message may be that matters, it's having the courage of One's faith when daring to seek "its" meaning that counts. The "thing" of "it" is - you've already been here before. And... en-light of that, this should be no big "thing" to recall.

Imagine that ... And "it" will soon appear.

Ha... Whapuuuuuu...

Peace and Courage to all beings of the realm

Aigh…

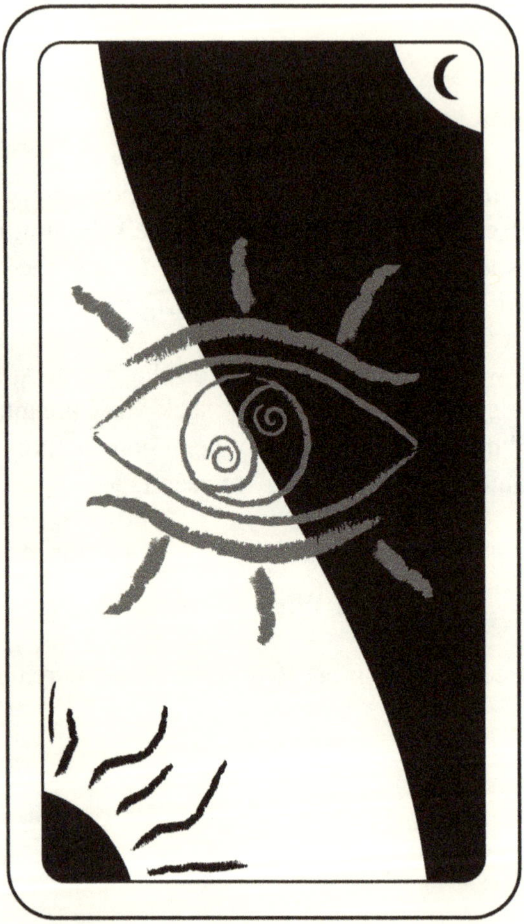

Wild Eye 2: Balanced Eye

Sub-deck: Wild Eyes

Wild Eye 2

Balanced Eye

Whapuuuuuu... Ha...

Another: Hey, Aigh've only got a minute - Aigh'm in the busyness of the stickiness of getting every-thing done. Some-thing like this takes time out of my chaotic day, and I don't think I can manage one more "thing."

Sure... "I kno" that no-thing like this can be planned for, "things" like this just randomly happen. And... I'm afraid "I don't kno" the reason why. With "things" being what they are, it's no-wonder all Aigh need to do is take three slow deep breaths to regain my balance, broadening my perspective.

Whapuuuuuu... Ha... Whapuuuuuu... Ha...
Whapuuuuuu... Ha...

One: Aigh get "it" may sound crazy at first, but the "thing" of "it" is, ya gotta have enough faith of your own to see "it" in this way to begin with. Balance in YinYang is a common "thing," which is a G_od thing, any way Aigh choose to look at "it."

It's not knoing what the message may be that matters, it's having the courage of One's faith when daring to seek "its" meaning that counts. The "thing" of "it" is - you've already been here before. And... en-light of that, this should be no big "thing" to recall.

Imagine that ... And "it" will soon appear.

Ha... Whapuuuuuu...

Peace and Courage to all beings of the realm

Aigh…

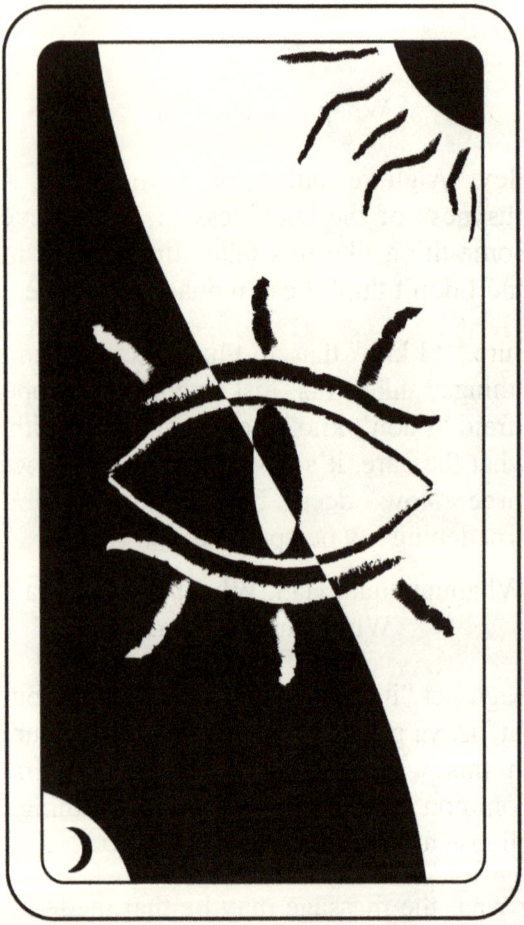

Wild Eye 3: Crazy Eye

Sub-deck: Wild Eyes

Wild Eye 3

Crazy Eye

Whapuuuuuu... Ha...

It's kind of crazy how many different ways there are to look at something like this. This could be no-thing but non-sense to some. While to others, every-thing makes enough sense that looking further only seems natural. Kind of like, Aigh kno this, it's not knoing that makes sense here. No-wonder is the reason why there's a chasm between OneAnother. And... counter to what the judge thinks, no One said every-thing was "right" in the realm. There are those "things" that run counter to what I think is right, and wonder is one of them.

For some, daring to wander there, wondering what's next, free from fearing what "I don't kno" about this reflection in front of me, is what led you to hear this moment in time.

It's not knoing what the message may be that matters, it's having the courage of One's faith when daring to seek "its" meaning that counts. The "thing" of "it" is - you've already been here before. And... en-light of that, this should be no big "thing" to recall.

Imagine that ... And "it" will soon appear.

Ha... Whapuuuuuu...

Peace and Courage to all beings of the realm

Aigh…

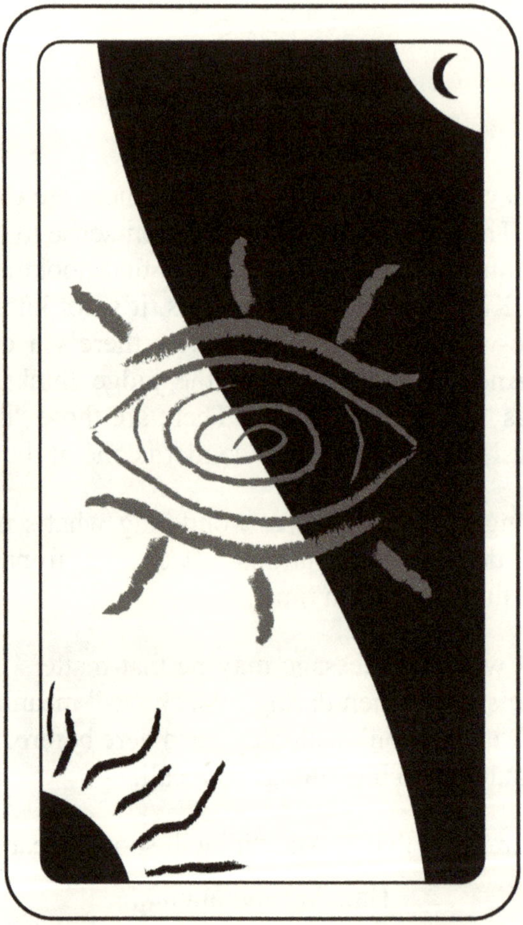

Wild Eye 4: Dizzy Eye

Sub-deck: Wild Eyes

Wild Eye 4

Dizzy Eye

Whapuuuuuu... Ha...

Another: Every-thing is spinning around me. "I don't kno" what's now, much less what's next, Aigh'm just praying that Aigh catch a break. Ya kno... just some-thing to point the way so the days don't just blur by. Running here, running there, as the deadlines form this meaningless trail behind me. "I kno I don't kno" a "thing" about this, and what I fear is what is not knoing to me.

One: It is at this place One sees the cycling of "things" that only a Balanced Eye sees with calm breath. As this reading spins through your insight, kno that your outlook is a breath away from seeing some-thing beyond what you can think to imagine.

It's not knoing what the message may be that matters, it's having the courage of One's faith when daring to seek "its" meaning that counts. The "thing" of "it" is - you've already been here before. And... en-light of that, this should be no big "thing" to recall.

Imagine that ... And "it" will soon appear.

Ha... Whapuuuuuu...

Peace and Courage to all beings of the realm

Aigh…

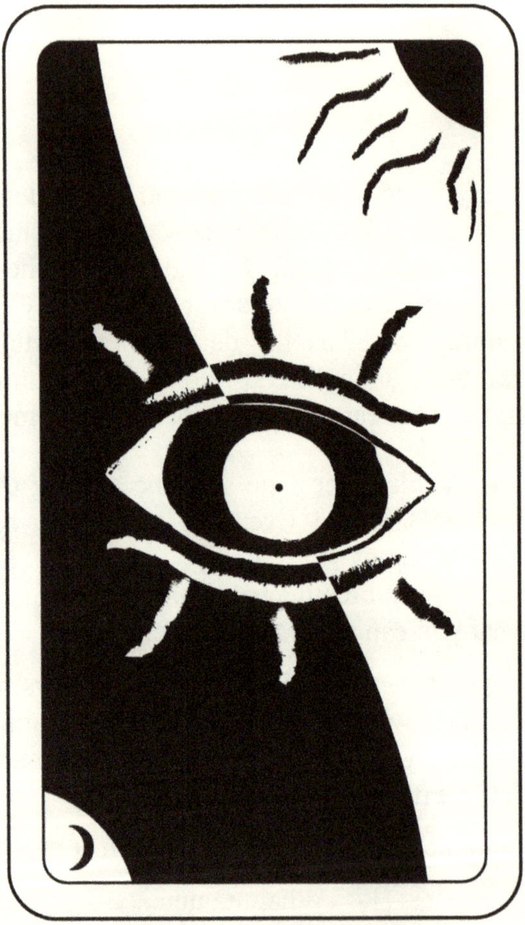

Wild Eye 5: Bright Eye

Sub-deck: Wild Eyes

Wild Eye 5

Bright Eye

Whapuuuuuu... Ha...

Ever alert, Bright Eye learns the ways of the realm for itself. Not knoing comes easy to the un-jaded, they haven't been taught what to fear. All souls kno the Bright Eye, we see it in our young. And if One lets go just enough, some-thing in this reading will catch the Bright Eye of One's soul once again.

It's not knoing what the message may be that matters, it's having the courage of One's faith when daring to seek "its" meaning that counts. The "thing" of "it" is - you've already been here before. And... en-light of that, this should be no big "thing" to recall.

Imagine that ... And "it" will soon appear.

Ha... Whapuuuuuu...

Peace and Courage to all beings of the realm

Aigh…

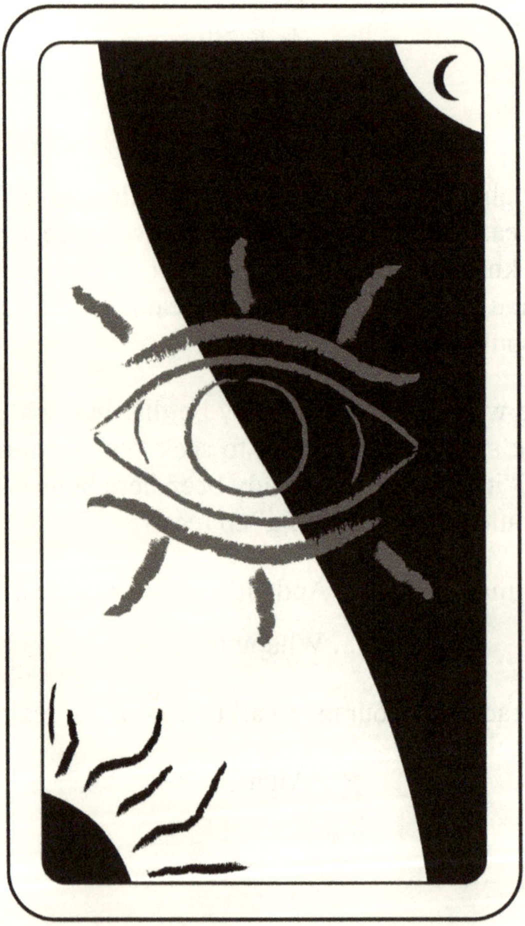

Wild Eye 6: Clear Eye

Sub-deck: Wild Eyes

Wild Eye 6

Clear Eye

Whapuuuuuu... Ha...

Clear Eye is the One who sees the trees of the forest with a knoing sense of where "it" is in the realm. Clear Eye is not phased by a dark moon's cycle, for it knos the light of day is present for those who look for the dawning, not knoing what it will look or sound like. Reading between the lines naturally, Clear Eye gets the message and takes it to One's heart.

It's not knoing what the message may be that matters, it's having the courage of One's faith when daring to seek "its" meaning that counts. The "thing" of "it" is - you've already been here before. And... en-light of that, this should be no big "thing" to recall.

Imagine that ... And "it" will soon appear.

Ha... Whapuuuuuu...

Peace and Courage to all beings of the realm

Aigh…

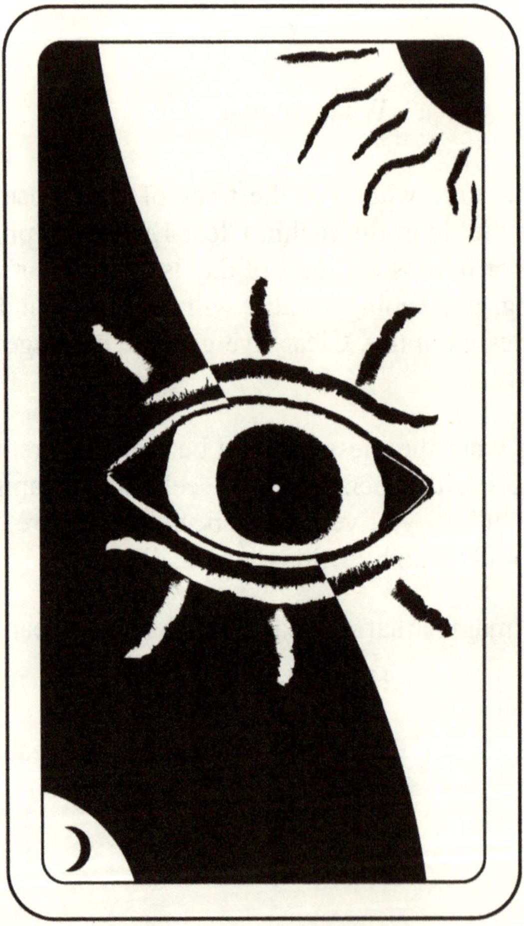

Wild Eye 7: Shadowed Eye

Sub-deck: Wild Eyes

Wild Eye 7

Shadowed Eye

Whapuuuuuu... Ha...

At the height of a moon's full presence in the realm lies the Shadowed Eye. Larger than its other, it is attracted to a darker sense of "things." All souls can sense its presents. Dark humor sounds smoother, the joke in reflection of those who think this is about control. The mirror thought of losing "it" is what shades One's agenda when planning to see "things" their way. It's not knoing… if One's worst fears will come insight, it's trusting a light breath of faith as you face "it" that will count.

Whapuuuuuu... Ha...

It's not knoing what the message may be that matters, it's having the courage of One's faith when daring to seek "its" meaning that counts. The "thing" of "it" is - you've already been here before. And... en-light of that, this should be no big "thing" to recall.

Imagine that ... And "it" will soon appear.

Ha... Whapuuuuuu...

Peace and Courage to all beings of the realm

Aigh…

Wild Eye 15: Skeptic's Eye

Sub-deck: Wild Eyes

Wild Eye 15

Skeptic's Eye

Whapuuuuuu... Ha...

Another: Ok... you kno me. "I kno" I don't trust any-thing without some-thing of proof. I'm open enough to listen to different "things," but these "things" called readings are just random suggestions, thoughts, and poems that don't add up in any way I can think of. No-wonder it takes faith to work with these "things," no-thing is clear that I can see. I'm afraid this is just a waste of my time, breath and energy.

One: It's not knoing if its gaze will be focused upon, or stemming from you, it's the courage to face One's reflection in the mirror that will make the difference when recalling what took place. Skeptic is the Eye of the wounded believer.

It's not knoing what the message may be that matters, it's having the courage of One's faith when daring to seek "its" meaning that counts. The "thing" of "it" is - you've already been here before. And... en-light of that, this should be no big "thing" to recall.

Imagine that ... And "it" will soon appear.

Ha... Whapuuuuuu...

Peace and Courage to all beings of the realm

Aigh…

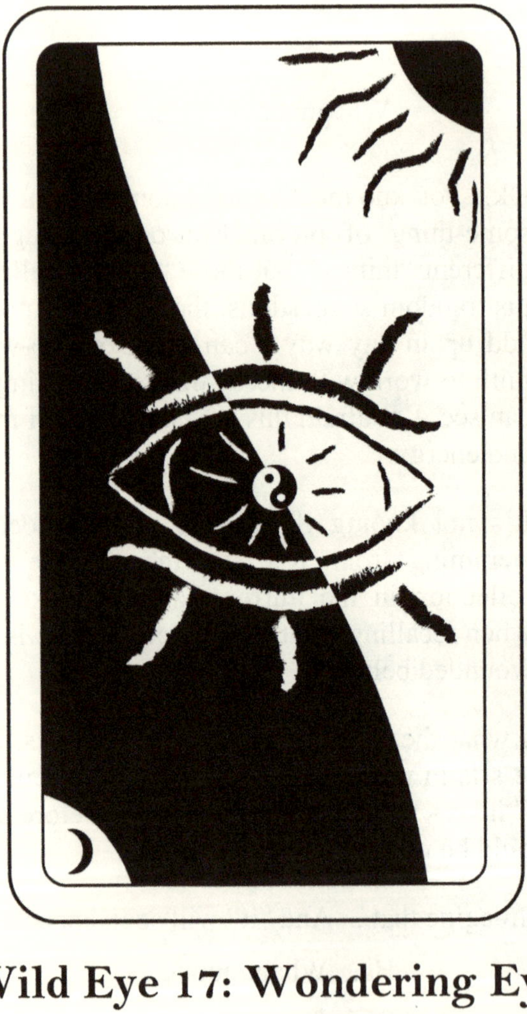

Wild Eye 17: Wondering Eye

Sub-deck: Wild Eyes

Wild Eye 17

Wondering Eye

Whapuuuuuu... Ha...

One: Daring to wander beyond what One can think to imagine, Wondering Eye is the looking glass to what's next. Coming to a knoing sense, not knoing every-thing is no-thing to fear - as some-thing like faith is One's "thing" to cling to, when a breath is all One can manage in the moment. Whapuuuuuu… Ha...

Life can change on a dime, the Wondering Eye sees the way to getting two nickels' worth of insight, rendering its outlook altered, in light of the experience.

Another: Knoing "what's at risk?" is some-thing I may think, no-thing "I kno" for sure, seeing every-thing insightfully, beyond what I could think to imagine before. Do Aigh dare to look?

One: It's not knoing... all spirits really do choose.

Another: No-wonder Aigh'm smiling in reflection of a reading like this, it would be what's next in YinYang, to what I thought was "right" about the readings of these "things," in the first place.

One: It's not knoing what the message may be that matters, it's having the courage of One's faith when daring to seek "its" meaning that counts. The "thing" of "it" is - you've already been here before. And... en-light of that, this should be no big "thing" to recall.

Imagine that ... And "it" will soon appear.

Ha... Whapuuuuuu...

Peace and Courage to all beings of the realm

Aigh…

Journaling Page

SCORE CARD

No-thing of Value	Some-thing of Value	Every-thing Between		CARD NAME	
☐	☐	☐	Yang	Entrance Portal	
☐	☐	☐	Yang	Guest Reading	
☐	☐	☐	Yang	Introduction	
☐	☐	☐	Yang	Is This Religious?	
☐	☐	☐	Yang	Crazy Buffalo's Reading	
☐	☐	☐	Yin	Well, hello Alice...	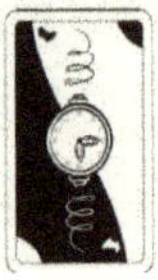
☐	☐	☐	Yang		
☐	☐	☐	Yang	Dealing with 39 cards	
☐	☐	☐	Yang	One Card Reading	

SCORE CARD

	CARD NAME		No-thing of Value	Some-thing of Value	Every-thing Between
	Three Card Reading	Yang	☐	☐	☐
	Five Card Reading	Yang	☐	☐	☐
	Wild Eye Reading	Yang	☐	☐	☐
	Crystal Healing for the Third-Eye Chakra	Yin	☐	☐	☐
		Yang	☐	☐	☐
	Illusion #1	Yin	☐	☐	☐
		Yang	☐	☐	☐
	No-thing of Value	Yin	☐	☐	☐
		Yang	☐	☐	☐
	Some-thing of Value	Yin	☐	☐	☐
		Yang	☐	☐	☐
	Every-thing Between	Yin	☐	☐	☐
		Yang	☐	☐	☐

SCORE CARD

No-thing of Value	Some-thing of Value	Every-thing Between		CARD NAME	
☐	☐	☐	Yin	Yin Meditation	
☐	☐	☐	Yang	Yang Meditation	
☐	☐	☐	Yang	YinYang Meditation	
☐	☐	☐	Yang	Cheat Sheet	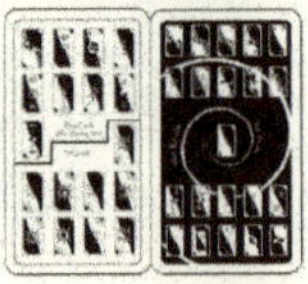
☐	☐	☐	Yang	Yin-Yang	
☐ ☐	☐ ☐	☐ ☐	Yin Yang	Breath of an Everyday Notion	
☐	☐	☐	Yang	Knowing the Future Exists	
☐ ☐	☐ ☐	☐ ☐	Yin Yang	Chaos of Ego's I	

SCORE CARD

	CARD NAME		No-thing of Value	Some-thing of Value	Every-thing Between
	T.S. Eliot's Truth	Yin	☐	☐	☐
		Yang	☐	☐	☐
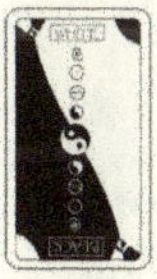	It's a Black & White "thing" No-wonder!	Yin	☐	☐	☐
		Yang	☐	☐	☐
	OK, five words or less	Yin	☐	☐	☐
		Yang	☐	☐	☐
	What was, what may be & what is	Yin	☐	☐	☐
		Yang	☐	☐	☐
	Wondering beyond what I think I kno is right	Yin	☐	☐	☐
		Yang	☐	☐	☐
	Common Thread	Yang	☐	☐	☐
	Man's World	Yang	☐	☐	☐
	What makes a man?	Yang	☐	☐	☐

SCORE CARD

No-thing of Value	Some-thing of Value	Every-thing Between		CARD NAME	
☐	☐	☐	Yin	Third-Eye's Insight	
☐	☐	☐	Yang		
☐	☐	☐	Yang	A recollection of space and time	
☐	☐	☐	Yang	Dawn of what's next	
☐	☐	☐	Yang	Fire	
☐	☐	☐	Yang	For fear of darkness or fear of light?	
☐	☐	☐	Yang	Silent Judge	
☐	☐	☐	Yang	The Dreamer	
☐	☐	☐	Yin	Good or God?	
☐	☐	☐	Yang		

SCORE CARD

	CARD NAME		No-thing of Value	Some-thing of Value	Every-thing Between
	I kno	Yin	☐	☐	☐
		Yang	☐	☐	☐
	I don't kno	Yin	☐	☐	☐
		Yang	☐	☐	☐
	Not knoing...	Yin	☐	☐	☐
		Yang	☐	☐	☐
	Knoing	Yin	☐	☐	☐
		Yang	☐	☐	☐
	Knock... Knock...	Yin	☐	☐	☐
		Yang	☐	☐	☐
	Clean Slate	Yin	☐	☐	☐
		Yang	☐	☐	☐
	Insightout	Yin	☐	☐	☐
		Yang	☐	☐	☐
	Sense of Balance	Yin	☐	☐	☐
		Yang	☐	☐	☐

SCORE CARD

No-thing of Value	Some-thing of Value	Every-thing Between		CARD NAME	
☐	☐	☐	Yin	Whapuuuuuu… Ha…	
☐	☐	☐	Yang		
☐	☐	☐	Yin	Non-Sense	
☐	☐	☐	Yang		
☐	☐	☐	Yin	Origin-al Eye	
☐	☐	☐	Yang		
☐	☐	☐	Yin	Balanced Eye	
☐	☐	☐	Yang		
☐	☐	☐	Yin	Crazy Eye	
☐	☐	☐	Yang		
☐	☐	☐	Yin	Dizzy Eye	
☐	☐	☐	Yang		
☐	☐	☐	Yin	Bright Eye	
☐	☐	☐	Yang		
☐	☐	☐	Yin	Clear Eye	
☐	☐	☐	Yang		

SCORE CARD

	CARD NAME		No-thing of Value	Some-thing of Value	Every-thing Between
	Shadowed Eye	Yin	☐	☐	☐
		Yang	☐	☐	☐
	Skeptic's Eye	Yin	☐	☐	☐
		Yang	☐	☐	☐
	Wondering Eye	Yin	☐	☐	☐
		Yang	☐	☐	☐
	SCORE CARD	Yang	☐	☐	☐
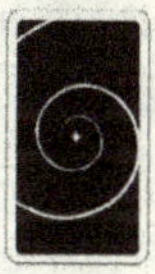	Quick Start Guide	Yang	☐	☐	☐

Quick Start Guide

1) When using this material, it is recommended that the user create an environment where s/he will not be disturbed or distracted. This product is for entertainment purposes and personal use only and is distributed "as is" without warranties of any kind.

2) What you will need: Image of Reflection materials, a journal, a Score Card and some time and G_od faith of your own. This Book of Cards is all you need to begin, however more cards, audio and other Image of Reflection materials are available online in the Realm's Bazaar: www.realmsbazaar.com

3) Too much of this stuff is just that, too much; so to start it is suggested that you read or listen to no more than 3 cards at a time.

4) Clearing ritual: Before beginning each reading session find a comfortable seating position, relax your neck and shoulders, close your eyes taking 3 long, slow, deep breaths to clear, cleanse and settle yourself, letting go of the "things" that you are carrying or feel burdened with. This is KEY when gazing into One's mirror reflection seeking insight. Failing to do so will cloud One's vision; where conversely the more One lets go, the clearer "things" begin to get.

5) To begin: Read/listen (download audio or online) to all of the Reference Cards in order as outlined. These cards are to give the work some structure to start with, but will become active cards of the deck later.

6) If you are reading these for yourself they are meant to be read aloud to One's "self" so you can hear the truth spoken in the sound of your own voice as you hear "it" said aloud. It doesn't sound like it would make that much difference, but counter to what Ego's I "thinks," it makes all the difference in the world – no wonder!

7) When you are ready to start the 39 card Starter Deck you have a choice to make. The cards can be read many ways but for now we'll start with two different ways.

   A) Consecutive order: Reading the cards as laid out in order is the shortest/fastest way through the work. This is the only way One can and will experience the work like someone else. Follow the same trail and end up in the same place - dazed and confused! Imagine that... This method is as cookie cutter as any other book off the shelf; however it is the safest and surest route to a timely end.

   B) Random order: Take your cards in hand then deal them for your-self and let the cards fall as they will. This way will ensure a one of a kind journey through the cards.

      Score Card is the key to giving this process some structure as One steps lightly into the realm not knoing... what's next.

      Keep track of the cards to ensure you get to them all in 31 to 93 days. Also be sure to listen to both the male/female readings. Keep track of the cards as they are read by scoring each one for the first 3 times they "come up." Aigh recommend using 3 different colored pens to score the cards each time you read them and keep the colors consistent (i.e. orange for all first cards, green for all second and purple for all third cards).

      First time a card turns up: Use one color to score the card.

      Second time a card turns up: Choose the male/female reading (whichever one you haven't heard already). Use a different color to score the card.

      Third time a card turns up: Choose between the male/female reading for your-self. Use a third color for notations.

      Reading the cards this way there are more reading combinations then One could possibly hear in 6 human life times so play with the randomness but focus on hearing all the readings. Sitting with all the cards is key to looking deeper into the deck as a whole.

If this is your first exposure to this body of work try to relax, letting your mind wonder along with the readings. They may sound like craziness at first... this is normal and to be expected. Truth is it only takes one card to open a Third Eye's insight. Trouble is, it's also not knoing which one it will be that does the trick. It's different for everyone; others may awaken to the same card as you, but their journey will randomly diverge from that point forward.

Don't worry about what combinations of cards mean or if cards are tending to repeat in pattern. Kno that anyone and everyone who has ever tested, worked on or played with the cards in one form or another has had patterns develop while they were handling them, it's to be expected along the way. When a pattern develops keep track of the card/cards and its/their orientation as it can be discussed online in one of the groups in the social realm at www.imaginariumofreflection.com

8) The Score Card serves a number of purposes but mainly it's used to track your progress through the cards by rendering a score along the way for each. The cards have many facets and everyone's insights differ regarding the score so individual scoring has meaning to the individual but not to anyone else. You're collecting a "heart of your truth" kind of scoring so there are no right or wrong answers. Whichever one is true in the moment for you is the "right" answer that should be scored. Kno that no One is supposed to "like" them all. "It" wouldn't be "real" if "things" were to appear all rosy each reading, now would it?

9) Doing anything every day is not only hard, but it becomes a chore to do. When Aigh read cards Aigh typically do it 3 at a time every 2 or 3 days, allowing time for insights to fully develop. Aigh mention this because many readers have found 1 card is not enough and more than 3 on average is too much. You'll figure this out for yourself, again personal preference. Try to spend 10-15 minutes on each card between reading/listening/journaling. Building a crisp discipline like this will help keep your ear in tune to the insights as they arise. Quick, simple notes are your keys to the reading; you can compile details later. The point is to document the reading's highlights; what comes to mind as connections are made may take a little time to gel. Make sense?

10) Journaling: So, why journal? Well, this is your personal road map through the cards. Like life at some point you're going to wonder; "How did Aigh get here?" Your journal will light the way; coming to an answer to that question is for you to recall for your-self. If written in G_od faith, it'll be a mirror reflection of you. Later it will become reflections of you that loved Ones may seek answers from for themselves, should you choose to share in the end. Each One of us has a story to tell; the cards serve to bring that story to mind with their reflections. Safeguard this for your-self, writing "things" down many times is the precursor to putting them down in a G_od way.

11) Questions? You are never alone in the realm of G_od faith – truth. Seek out a group online or start one of your own in the social realm at: www.imaginariumofreflection.com

    Cards, audio and other Image of Reflection materials are available online in the Realm's Bazaar at: www.realmsbazaar.com

12) And… if you're wondering why the Quick Start Guide is at the end of this "thing," well, that's easy. Those who came looking for some instruction quickly found the guide in the index, flipped to the end then simply started "what's next." Still others may not come to read "it" until they've reached the end of this non-sense due to what they think at the onset. It's not knoing… *how* One gets to the end that matters; it's getting a quick start onto what's next *beyond* the end that will count up ahead. Some come dying to get there, thinking the shortest route is the wisest… plunging right in, it's no-wonder that here at the end of "it" all lies the start of what's next. Still others may hang on for dear life choosing to see "what's next" only after the end actually comes. Seeing every-thing flashing before their eyes it's no-wonder the pattern of life seems like it just keeps repeating itself, like déjà-vu all over again-n-again-n-again… Dying to break the cycle, "it" is here at the end that all "things" begin anew.

What's at the end of this? It's not knoing… getting to kno the peace, love and joy of "it" is the treasure that awaits. Starting with the end in mind is always the quickest way to encounter a G_od sense for your-self. Fore in the realm all spirits really do choose for themselves - it would be what's next.

Imagine that… and "it" will soon appear.

Ha… Whapuuuuuu...

Peace and Courage to all beings of the realm

Aigh...

Migh heartfelt gratitude goes to

Migh wife & sons
Jakie & Miss Millie
Migh Mom, Dad, & siblings
Bill & Othella Adcock & family

And to all those who Aigh've connected with through the years who were part of the millions of random events to have touched migh life along the way to coming to this body of work.

Peace, Love and Joy to each and every One of you.

Aigh…

About the Author

Joshua, Roger, Taylor Egner

Migh name is Roger Egner and Aigh am Crazy Buffalo. Eight years ago Aigh began writing a deck of spiritual Oracle Cards based on the Tao Te Ching. Aigh was in the 43rd year of migh being, in the 18th year of migh marriage and in the stresses and duresses of mid-life. Aigh had two sons in the prime of their teenage years and had recently relocated cross-country. Aigh was lost in the process of figuring out what to do with migh-self in this new time-n-place, having taken care of everyone else.

For years Aigh had been a reader of Tarot and Spiritual Oracle cards when seeking insight for migh-self. I had never envisioned myself writing anything, much less a deck of Oracle cards. Truth is, writing wasn't migh thing back then and had you asked me, I would've told you a story all about "it."

"It" did make me wonder though what kind of experience it would take/be to create an Oracle deck of cards. So Aigh set out to find out just what it would "be" to accomplish this task. The next "thing" Aigh recall is waking up on a carpet humbled from a fall. Aigh had crossed the line and lived to speak of "it." So Aigh did, with a Zen Priest. Aigh queried, "Where do Aigh begin?" He replied with a laughing howl, "Why at the beginning, where else?!" and pointed me to the Tao. I asked, "What's this "thing" all about?" He howled even louder saying, "It's not knoing… you're going to love it!" Migh sons are naturally closer to the origin than Aigh given our places in life so Aigh looked to them for their insights upon reading "it." It was then that the cards began to flow from each One of us.

Image of Reflection™ and the Mirror™ Cards that make up the realm were all channeled in G_od faith. From where or from who is not knoing… any-thing more would be pure speculation. That is the truth as Aigh've come to kno "it." And… as crazy as that may sound at first the harmonic balance that is a natural by-product of "it" is some-thing to behold in this life.

"It's" written in the cards for each One of us to come to this place naturally. You don't have to be G_od at playing games to come out a winner in the realm. All One needs is the courage and faith enough of your own to gaze into the looking glass. What's next in mirror reflection is not knoing… On the other side of that, it's for you to choose. Fore in the realm all spirits really do choose for themselves – it's what's next!

Imagine that… and "it" will soon appear.

Peace and Courage to all beings of the realm

Aigh…

Gates of the Realm
Social realm
Reader's realm
the Realm's Bazaar
Image of Reflection™

Mirror Card Index

www.ingramcontent.com/pod-product-compliance
Lightning Source LLC
Chambersburg PA
CBHW021056090426
42738CB00006B/360
* 9 7 8 0 5 7 8 0 8 0 8 1 9 *